The Total Teacher

What are the keys to thriving as an educator? This insightful book from bestselling author Danny Steele reveals how the most effective teachers are well-rounded and three-dimensional: (1) grounded in the technical side (classroom management, instruction, and professional growth); (2) dedicated to the relationship work (the purpose of what we do); and (3) committed to the vital role they play in building the school's culture. The book is organized into three parts, one for each dimension, and provides strategies, inspirational stories, and helpful examples from educators who are doing the work. Perfect for new and experienced teachers, this unique book will help you reflect on the art of being a teacher so you can enhance your professional practice.

Danny Steele (@steelethoughts) is a principal from Birmingham, Alabama, and has worked in public education for over 27 years. In 2016, he was named Alabama's Secondary Principal of the Year. He has presented at numerous state and national conferences, and writes an educational leadership blog that has received over 5 million page views.

T0386584

Also Available from Routledge Eye On Education
(www.routledge.com/k-12)

Essential Truths for Principals
Danny Steele and Todd Whitaker

Essential Truths for Teachers
Danny Steele and Todd Whitaker

Education Write Now, Volume I
Edited by Jeffrey Zoul and Joe Mazza

Education Write Now, Volume II: Top Strategies for Improving Relationships and Culture
Edited by Jeffrey Zoul and Sanée Bell

Education Write Now, Volume III: Solutions to Common Challenges in Your School or Classroom
Edited by Jeffrey Zoul and Sanée Bell

The Total Teacher

Understanding the Three Dimensions that Define Effective Educators

Danny Steele

Routledge
Taylor & Francis Group

NEW YORK AND LONDON

First published 2022
by Routledge
605 Third Avenue, New York, NY 10158

and by Routledge
2 Park Square, Milton Park, Abingdon, Oxon, OX14 4RN

Routledge is an imprint of the Taylor & Francis Group, an Informa business

© 2022 Taylor & Francis

The right of Danny Steele to be identified as author of this work has been asserted by him in accordance with sections 77 and 78 of the Copyright, Designs and Patents Act 1988.

Trademark notice: Product or corporate names may be trademarks or registered trademarks, and are used only for identification and explanation without intent to infringe.

Library of Congress Cataloging-in-Publication Data
Names: Steele, Danny, author.
Title: The total teacher : understanding the three dimensions that define effective educators / Danny Steele.
Description: New York, NY : Routledge, 2021. | Series: Routledge eye on education | Includes bibliographical references. | Identifiers: LCCN 2021004624 (print) | LCCN 2021004625 (ebook) | ISBN 9780367622527 (hardback) | ISBN 9780367478421 (paperback) | ISBN 9781003108566 (ebook)
Subjects: LCSH: Effective teaching. | Classroom management. | Teachers--Professional relationships. | School environment.
Classification: LCC LB1025.3 .S73433 2021 (print) | LCC LB1025.3 (ebook) | DDC 371.102--dc23
LC record available at https://lccn.loc.gov/2021004624
LC ebook record available at https://lccn.loc.gov/2021004625

ISBN: 978-0-367-62252-7 (hbk)
ISBN: 978-0-367-47842-1 (pbk)
ISBN: 978-1-003-10856-6 (ebk)

Typeset in Palatino
by SPi Global, India

This book is dedicated to all the "total teachers" I have worked with in my career—and there are many! Thank you for your commitment to your craft, to your students, and to your colleagues. You have inspired me.

Contents

Meet the Author

Dr. Danny Steele is a principal from Birmingham, Alabama, and has worked in public education for over 27 years. In addition to serving as a principal at multiple levels, he has worked as a teacher, coach, assistant principal, and university instructor. In 2005, Danny was recognized as the Secondary Assistant Principal of the Year for the state of Alabama, and in 2016, he was named Alabama's Secondary Principal of the Year. He has presented at numerous state and national conferences, and he writes an educational leadership blog that has received over 5 million page views. Danny has an undergraduate degree in History from Covenant College (Lookout Mountain, GA); he has an M.A. in History from the University of Alabama, Birmingham; he has an Educational Specialist degree in Educational Administration and an Educational Doctorate degree in Educational Leadership, both from Samford University. He lives with his wife, Holley, in Birmingham, Alabama. They have three children; DJ, Will, and Elizabeth.

Acknowledgements

The poet, John Donne, wrote that "No man is an island." This famous line speaks to the truth of the connections that we share with one another. We don't live in a vacuum; we don't work in a vacuum; and authors don't write books in a vacuum. There is a context for everything that we do, and we are remiss when we don't acknowledge it. I've always appreciated it when I see a running back who has just scored a touchdown hand the ball to his offensive lineman to spike. I appreciate the recognition that he did not succeed on his own. When any of us succeeds, it is because there are others who have helped us along the way. There are many individuals who have helped me on my journey as an educator and an author, but I want to highlight just a few here.

Thanks to my editor, Lauren Davis, and her team at Routledge. She has been tremendously supportive, and her keen editorial eye has made this a stronger book. I am grateful for her believing in my message.

I appreciate the collaboration, support, and endless wisdom I have received from Todd Whitaker. My conversations with him helped me to clarify my thinking about the structure of this book.

I have worked with many amazing educators in my career, but I want to acknowledge two in particular. I have had the privilege of working alongside Neely Woodley and Cas McWaters. Over the years, I have spent countless hours talking with them about the art of teaching. They were great teachers and are currently inspiring educational leaders. I have always valued their collaboration and friendship.

My brother, David, has always believed in me as a teacher, as an administrator, and as an author. Words are not adequate for how thankful I am for his relentless encouragement.

And to my wife, Holley… thank you for supporting me as I pursued this passion. Thank you for sharing my excitement when I would come home from work and talk about the inspiring work of our teachers. Thank you for reading all the drafts of this book and providing thoughtful feedback. Thank you for being my greatest cheerleader. Thank you for always being in my corner. Thank you for being on this journey with me.

Author's Note

Portions of this book are drawn from some of my earlier writing, including blogs, *Essential Truths for Teachers*, and *Education Write Now: Volume III*.

Introduction

If you graduate from medical school, you will be addressed as "Dr." When you complete your residency, you can start practicing medicine. You will be a doctor. But that does not mean you will be a good one. When we have to get medical help, we surely have higher hopes for the physician treating us than that their diploma on the wall is not a forgery. And we usually hope for more than just mere "competence." When we are looking for a doctor—and certainly when we are taking a loved one for medical care— we are not looking for adequate care; we're looking for excellent care. We do not want the medical professional treating us to be average; we want them to be exceptional. While I am not an authority on medical care, let me propose that there are three facets to medical care that define excellent doctors.

First, they understand the technical side of medical practice. They paid attention in medical school and learned the material. They understand the body and know how it works. They can recognize symptoms and know what symptoms go with what ailment. They are familiar with the best way to treat diseases, and they know which drugs to prescribe in which circumstances. They read medical journals, and attend conferences to stay current on the latest research and the most effective therapeutic techniques. In layman's terms, they know their stuff.

Second, the most effective doctors appreciate the human component of medical practice. A line from the Hippocratic Oath, reads: "I will remember that there is art to medicine as well as science, and that warmth, sympathy, and understanding may outweigh the surgeon's knife or the chemist's drug." This is what we refer to as "bedside manner." It is a quality that every patient appreciates in their doctor. Another line from the Oath reads: "I will remember that I do not treat a fever chart, a cancerous growth, but a sick human being, whose illness may affect the person's family and economic stability. My responsibility includes these related problems, if I am to care adequately for the sick." When we see the doctor, we want them to listen to us and to genuinely care. We want them to show compassion. While these qualities make the experience more enjoyable for us, good doctors understand that taking the time to listen to and understand the patient generally leads to a higher level of treatment.

And, finally, medicine is never practiced in a vacuum; there is a cultural context that ultimately impacts total quality of care. Great doctors recognize that they don't know it all. Taking another line from the Hippocratic Oath: "I will not be ashamed to say 'I know not' nor will I fail to call on my colleagues when the skills of another are needed for a patient's recovery." Many times doctors will ask for a second opinion on reading a scan. Or they will discuss with a colleague the best way to approach a particularly complicated surgery. And it is certainly common for a team of doctors to lean on each other as they determine the best path of treatment for a cancer victim. But it is more than just a willingness to collaborate. The culture of a hospital has an impact on the quality of care that its patients enjoy. It affects the attitudes and practices of nurses, technicians, and a host of other assistants. Anyone who has been in a hospital or sat with a loved one can testify to this. They have felt it.

Hopefully, the quality control of medical schools and licensure boards ensures a basic level of competence that we can all take for granted when we visit a clinic, or check in at the local hospital. But is it possible for a doctor to practice medicine and not excel in all three facets discussed above? Sure. Can they adequately diagnose our illness, prescribe the right medicine, and still be a jerk in the process? Perhaps. Can they feel confident in their diagnosis without double-checking with colleagues? Maybe. Can they do their job without having a positive attitude? I suppose. But what kind of doctor do you think will be most effective? To which practice do you want to donate your copay? I think the answer is obvious.

Just as a medical degree does not make an effective doctor, a teaching certificate does not make an effective teacher. In this book, I want to make the case that, much like the most effective doctors, the most effective teachers—the most well-rounded teachers—are three-dimensional. Just as there is an "art" to the professional practice of medicine, there is an art to the professional practice of teaching.

As the exceptional physician is well-grounded in the technical side of medical practice, the exceptional teacher is well-versed in the technical areas of their profession. This is the first dimension. Chapter 1 discusses the approach to managing the classroom and the importance of handling student discipline in a constructive way. Chapter 2 describes the way in which teachers can build positive climates in their classroom and how this enhances instruction. Chapter 3 outlines the process of meaningful instruction, and dives into the nuts and bolts of teaching lessons. Chapter 4 highlights the important role that professional growth plays for the most effective educators and outlines four strategies for teachers to elevate their game.

The second dimension, relationships, gets to the heart of our profession and the core of why we do what we do—our students. Just as we want our doctors to have a good "bedside manner," our students and their parents hope their teachers have a good way with kids. Chapter 5 underscores the purpose of teachers. Chapter 6 elaborates on the importance of teachers knowing and understanding their students. And Chapter 7 provides examples for how teachers can approach the process of building relationships with their students.

The third dimension of outstanding teachers involves their ability to embrace their role as a contributing member of the faculty, and we explore this in Chapter 8. Just as physicians have the potential to shape the culture of a hospital, teachers have the ability to influence the collective attitudes, norms, values, and practices of a school. The best teachers are not victims of poor school culture; they help to build it. They commit to making their school a great place for kids to learn and adults to work.

This book is not meant to be an exhaustive account of the various elements of teaching. To be sure, authors have written books about facets of this profession to which I have devoted only a single paragraph. Rather, I intended this book to be an overview of what defines the most well-rounded teachers. My goal in writing this is to underscore in a concise way, yet with broad strokes, the core practices of teachers—teachers that principals like to lead and from whom students like to learn. These are the qualities and habits of effective educators. For veteran teachers, I hope you see yourself in these pages, and I hope this book validates the important work that you do. I also hope it inspires you to keep on keepin' on. For new teachers, I hope this work shines a light on your path. You learn quickly in your career that there is more to teaching than writing an innovative lesson plan. I hope this book serves as a guide as you embark on this awesome journey.

I am compelled here to point out that the three dimensions are not equivalent; they are not all equally important. Accordingly, the three dimensions are not each afforded the same number of chapters in this book. While I argue that all three dimensions are essential for *The Total Teacher*, they do not all carry the same weight. When it comes down to it, the *Technical Perspective* encompasses the fundamental practice of teachers. So, if you pinned me to the wall, I would propose this dimension is the most important; it deserves the most chapters. As every teacher knows, however, the instructional component cannot truly be divorced from the relational component. The relationships are crucial. So, I devote three chapters to this dimension. Good schools are predicated on strong cultures, and teachers play a valuable role here. The role teachers play in contributing to strong school culture is not necessarily the most important role they play, but it is still an essential piece in discussing the "total teacher," so I explore it in Chapter 8. These dimensions all work together, and they certainly have a significant amount of overlap. That being the case, I have still decided it is worthwhile to consider these dimensions in three distinct sections.

I will also note here that I have included a fourth dimension in the Epilogue, and it involves the importance of teachers taking care of themselves. Just as the medical profession would never want burned-out, jaded, and unrested doctors going into surgery, the education profession cannot afford to have stressed out, worn down, and uninspired teachers going into the classroom. So, I conclude the book with a brief discussion of the significance of teacher self-care.

I have worked with many extraordinary teachers in my career, and I am delighted that I can include some of their voices in this project. Each chapter will feature the first-hand words of teachers who are doing the *work*. It is my hope that these segments will add some credibility to the concepts in the book, as well as clarify what they look like in practice. On a personal level, I am thrilled that I can feature these teachers. I am honored to have called them colleagues, I have been inspired by their work, and I am profoundly grateful for their contributions.

Part I

The First Dimension

The Technical Perspective

1

Managing the Classroom

I remember a veteran teacher sharing with me his frustrations about his fifth-period class. He felt as though he had exhausted his bag of tricks, and students still were not cooperating. They didn't seem to care about his carrots OR his sticks. Finally, he quipped, "I just don't like 'em." I remember having classes like that, even when I felt as though I was good at classroom management. Most teachers, if they are honest, will admit that there have been some days, weeks, or even years, when a certain class got the better of them. And those classes can really leave a bad taste in your mouth. A particularly challenging group of students can ruin your day and, in some cases, make you question your profession.

Conventional wisdom maintains that classroom management is required before effective instruction can take place, and I suspect most educators could confirm the truth of this adage. Wang, Haertel, and Walberg (December 1993/January 1994) reviewed 50 years of research and found that classroom management had the single highest impact on student learning. Maintaining an orderly classroom and ensuring good student behavior is foundational. The teacher who shows up on the first day without a plan will undoubtedly find out just how foundational it is. So, we begin by focusing on classroom management, including the role of organization, routines, and student discipline.

Organization

Many experts have written about the ins and outs of classroom management, but none have made a bigger impact than *First Days of School* by Harry and Rosemary Wong (2005). Given the title of their book, it is not surprising that they write, "Your success during the school year will be determined by what you do the first days of school." (3) They talk about the importance of establishing control over the class through consistency and high expectations. They maintain that how your class looks, how you are dressed, how you communicate, and how well-prepared you are, all impact your level of effectiveness. They caution, "Nothing will send kids into orbit faster than letting them suspect that their teacher is disorganized." (84) According to the Wongs, the organized classroom is task oriented; there are clear expectations for students; and there is little wasted time. In these classrooms teachers prepare themselves, the learning space, and the learning materials.

In *The Organized Teacher*, Springer, Alexander, and Persiani (2012) provide an exhaustive checklist of supplies for teachers to make sure they have in their classrooms. They go on to provide examples of effective room setups, behavior charts, work center structures, filing systems, record keeping, and sub-folders.

I once had a colleague who had a bulletin board in his class that had group assignments for the nine weeks. Every time he wanted students in groups, everyone knew where to go and who was in their group. There was no wasted time during class organizing into groups, figuring out who was going where. It was an investment of the teacher's time at the beginning of each quarter, but this level of organization and preparation paid big dividends in saving instructional time throughout the year.

Routines

In some classrooms, there is a lot of wasted time. Teachers continually have to provide directions, and inevitably repeat themselves over and over again. In other classrooms, students walk into class and immediately begin working. They know the "drill."

Quite often, the varying levels of productivity within different classrooms can be attributed to the extent to which routines are in place. Routines are important. These are the ritual behaviors that have been taught and practiced from the beginning of the school year. These could include practices such as "bell-ringer" activities, procedures for collecting makeup work, and expectations for using classroom supplies. The younger the students, the more important and prevalent the routines. Kindergarteners for example, may have routines for washing hands, sitting on the floor, lining up for lunch, and walking down the hallway. It is important to remember that one size will never fit all. Routines that work for one teacher may seem cumbersome for another. Procedures that some teachers cannot live without may seem unwieldy to others. Early in my career I found a couple routines that worked for me. In my ninth-grade class, we had several jobs that rotated every nine weeks.

The first job was the timekeeper. I would often get carried away with my own teaching and lose track of time. The bell would ring, and I had not yet brought closure to the lesson, or even talked about the homework. So, I assigned one student to give me a discreet signal every day when there were two minutes left in class. I found these reminders to be quite helpful.

The second job entailed being responsible for making sure our class set of textbooks were all accounted for and back neatly on the shelf. If you have been in a classroom for any length of time, you already know that items can walk out of your room, intentionally or unintentionally. This accountability for keeping up with our books was invaluable.

Students who walk across the classroom to throw away trash right in the middle of class can disrupt the lesson. Moreover, it can be embarrassing when visitors to your class in the afternoon get to witness the mess that results as trash has accumulated on the floor from all your earlier classes. We remedied these concerns with our third job. At the point that our timekeeper signaled that class was wrapping up, and one student was counting textbooks, a third student was walking around with the trash can to collect what the students needed to throw away. As we went over these jobs on the first day, I explained to my students that,

"The bell does not dismiss you; I do." And I assured the students that I would dismiss the students immediately on the ringing of the bell as long as all the books were accounted for and there was no trash on the floor.

With a little training and practice, even young students can learn many different routines. My ninth-graders learned these expectations quickly; and I did not have to worry about the bell sneaking up on me; I did not have to worry about books walking out of the room; and my room stayed clean all day.

Student Behavior

For years, I have asked prospective teachers who are interviewing for a job a question like this: "What's the secret to good classroom management?" I usually get an answer such as: "Have a few clear rules posted in your room; communicate to your students at the beginning of the year what the consequences will be for the various infractions; and then be consistent in the enforcement of those rules." This is not a bad answer, even if it is predictable. For the 22-year-olds who are interviewing, this could have been a script they had regurgitated not too long before on a college exam. But there is more to it than that.

As an administrator, I have always noticed that students behaved in some classes but not in others. Kids could be model students in some classrooms but could be disruptive and disrespectful in others. That tells me that teachers have the ability to influence student behavior. More often than not, teachers are the variable. I do, of course, realize that the chemistry in certain classrooms can make a difference, and sometimes even the time of day can impact the level of hyperactivity of certain students. These variables notwithstanding, teachers have enormous potential to impact student behavior simply by how they interact with them.

As it turns out, the first essential step in effective classroom management... is actually liking the students in your room. Students are much more responsive to teachers who genuinely like them, and this often translates into better behavior. But the best classroom management is not about controlling the behavior; it's about winning over the kids—building personal connections. And we earn the respect of our students by how we treat them. Indeed, classroom management is not about having the right rules; it is about having the right relationships. Student discipline is so much easier when you have rapport with the kids. Getting to know your students truly does make all the difference. We also need to understand that when students act out, it is usually the result of an unmet need. Ginott (1972) noted, "Children often misbehave when they have difficulty with an assignment… A teacher's best antidote to misbehavior is a willingness to be helpful. (51) Punishing a student may address the behavior, but it does not meet the need. Sometimes students need consequences for their misbehavior, but it is not usually the consequences that change the behavior, and very seldom will this win the student over. If we don't get to the root of the misbehavior, it is unlikely that the punishment will solve the problem. Todd Whitaker (2012) writes, "Effective teachers want to prevent misbehavior, whereas ineffective teachers focus on punishing a student after he or she misbehaves. (25) Rather than focusing on managing kids, it works best when we try to understand them. It is also important to note that holding students accountable and demonstrating compassion are not mutually exclusive notions. You can always extend grace while you provide discipline. You can always respect the student's dignity while you administer consequences.

We will devote an entire chapter later in the book to the importance of knowing your students but, at this point in our discussion of managing student behavior, it is crucial that we address one aspect of understanding students. The noted psychologist Abraham Maslow (1943) outlined an innovative theory of human motivation in a model that he described as a "hierarchy of needs." Chances are good that you came across this theory as an undergraduate, and it has received copious attention over the decades in workshops, conferences, articles, and books. I suspect most teachers are familiar with this theory and, at an intuitive level, they get it. Maslow argued that we are all motivated to get certain needs met, and we don't focus on higher needs until we have first satisfied the more basic ones. In the classroom, students are not able to focus on the lesson if they are hungry. Students who do not feel as though they have a safe place to go home to after school will probably not be as diligent in their studies as their classmates who feel more "secure." This dynamic resonates with most teachers and, in fact, many might consider it common sense. In my experience, this is where the application of Maslow's hierarchy to the educational context often stops. But as a young assistant principal who spent most of his day handling disciplinary referrals, I came to realize that there was a facet to this theory that had significant implications for classroom management.

Imagine this scenario: The teacher tells the class, "Ok students... turn to page 276 and start answering the questions." (Ten seconds later, John turns around and begins talking to the student behind him.) The teacher notices this and says with a firm tone, "John, I said to get busy; now be quiet." And John responds with a bit of an edge to his voice: "I was just asking her for a pencil." The teacher retorts, "I don't care what you were asking her. You shouldn't be talking." John can't let it go. "You didn't say anything to Michael! He was talking too!" (And five minutes later, John is in the office with a disciplinary referral that says: "DISRUPTIVE and DISRESPECTFUL!)

So, what happened? Should John have come to class prepared? Of course. Should he have responded, "Yes sir" when admonished by his teacher? Indeed. But I'm afraid scenarios like this one are all too common in schools. As a general rule, students need consequences for inappropriate behavior. But it is also a general rule that students learn more sitting in the classroom than in the principal's office. So, if we can figure out how to avoid these scenarios, that is ideal. So, why could Dr. Maslow have predicted that it would play out the way it did? And how might this situation have been avoided?

More often than not, students care more about what their classmates think than what their teacher thinks. The need to maintain positive relationships with peers is right in the middle of Maslow's pyramid. So, the lesson here is don't put students in a position where they feel like they need to "save face." As Whitaker (2012) notes,

We never win an argument with a student. As soon as it starts, we have lost. If their peers are watching, they cannot afford to give in. We would like to win the argument, but they have to win the argument.

(28)

The Disrespectful Student

Think back to Maslow's pyramid and the scenario where John became disrespectful to his teacher after he felt embarrassed. And think about how many teachers might be tempted to respond to John's disrespect. "Don't use that tone with me, young man. I'm the teacher in here, and you just earned yourself a trip to the office!" As an assistant principal, I remember coming to the realization that Maslow's theory doesn't just apply to kids; it applies to adults, too. When a student is disrespectful, an insecure teacher may feel threatened; he or she may feel that their authority is being undermined in front of the class. That teacher may feel tempted to "put the student in her place." When I was a kid, I remember a slogan from a deodorant commercial: "Never let them see you sweat." That's a great mantra for teachers. Don't let the kids get to you. Marzano (2003) referred to it as "emotional objectivity." He argues, "An effective classroom manager implements and enforces rules and procedures, executes disciplinary actions, and cultivates effective relationships with students without becoming upset if students violate classroom rules and procedures... ." (94) Effective teachers stay at the top of their pyramid. Teachers with strong classroom management don't have to remind students who the "adult" is. The kids all figured that out the first day.

When a student is disrespectful, talk to them privately. Whispering to students who are out of line is actually a valuable strategy and one of the most practical management tips I can give teachers. When you whisper to students what you need them to do, more than likely you will get a positive response. This is because you have not embarrassed them. Whispering takes away the student's audience, and it eliminates the need to "save face." And don't take the disrespect personally; it is almost never the core issue. Rather, it is a symptom of something deeper. It is easy for the adults in the school to lose sight of that… but they can't.

So, here is an exercise: think of your most challenging student. Now think of how you might potentially interact with that student differently. Remember that one of the first steps in connecting with a challenging student is to *like* them, rather than "put up" with them. It is amazing how the attitude of the adult can affect the attitude of the student. I am not saying the student's misbehavior is the teacher's fault, but the approach of the adult is often a significant variable. If you want to succeed with a difficult student, you have to separate the attitude from the student. You don't lower your standards, but you understand that there is always something motivating the behavior. Understanding leads to empathy and empathy makes positive teacher–student relationships possible. Ultimately, kids do not want to be bad; they want to have their needs met. It's good when we can focus on understanding the students and meeting their needs, rather than just reacting to the "bad behavior."

> I have been asked several times, how was I able to "manage" my classrooms very early on in my teaching career. After 20 years of teaching, I have concluded that most of what I thought or was told about classroom management was really not what I did. I could tell you all of the "textbook" things that you should have in place. For example, have rules and procedures (for EVERYTHING), manage grading assignments and providing feedback in a timely manner, use small groups, rows, etc. Actually, although all of those things are great and needed, but they are not what I would consider the best classroom management tool I used. I simply cared enough to care! I cared about the well-being of my students more than I cared about my content. I had decided that if they knew that I actually cared about them (what happened in the neighborhood, how many points they scored at the game, how they performed on the test in another class), then I would

probably be able to get them to work for me in my class. How did I get them to know that I actually cared, by asking them one simple question, "What are your expectations of me as a teacher"? See, we were in it together and we ALL had to have buy in, set expectations, and follow through. My classrooms were simply never one sided.

Kassander Robinson, Teacher

In order to fully understand my teaching style, you must understand a normal day in our classroom. It is not quiet. Students are not still. There is a sense of security that allows even the most unsure students to feel like they can attack problems of great difficulty. We make mistakes, we learn from them, and we share those mistakes and lessons learned with each other. I fully believe that students need an environment that fosters risk taking, collaboration, and celebration of even the smallest of successes. At the beginning of our school year, our principal asked us to write our teaching oath. After much thought and many attempts at putting this on paper, I asked my students what qualities in a teacher best supported their success in school. They gave me the following: encouraging, celebrating, listening, supportive, helpful, fun, creative, unique, understanding, nice, smart, caring, considerate, "awesome-sauce," funny, energetic, and enthusiastic. This list stays posted outside my classroom door. I look at it each morning and make the decision to not only be what my students desire, but also what they need. I choose daily to go out of my way to make sure each student knows they are cared for and they have a cheerleader in their corner. If they feel secure in these ways, learning will happen. Academic progress comes from the confidence to try new and difficult tasks.

Amber Willis, Teacher

2

Creating the Climate

In all my years of conducting formal classroom observations, one of my favorites was in a ninth-grade math class. This was not just any math class, though; it was the lowest level of math that our school offered. So, you can imagine the students who were placed in this room. They had not had a lot of success with math in their school experiences, and most of them did not think math was for them. They lacked confidence with the subject and, frankly, many of those students found it intimidating.

This class period I was sitting in the back of the room, watching the lesson unfold. There was a lot of interaction between the teacher and students as one-by-one, kids were coming up to the front to work problems at the board. The teacher would ask questions about the problem, and students would shout out answers. And then I heard a student say something I will never forget. In the middle of the teacher affirming the myriad of correct answers coming from students, a girl blurted out: *"We're so smart!"*

So, think about that for a second. Consider why that little statement made such an impression on me. These were students who probably had not found many reasons to feel good about their academic achievement or their academic potential. Yet, this class defied my expectations. I encountered an environment and an attitude I had not anticipated. The positive energy in this classroom was palpable. The students were engaged and interactive.

And they had confidence. They felt good about their learning and about their contributions to the class. So, what made this classroom unique. What was the variable?

The difference was Coach Hamlin. The difference was the climate he created in his room. There is an abundance of research that testifies to the fact that climate in the classroom plays an important role in the level of learning that takes place (Schweig, Hamilton, & Baker, 2019). And any administrator who has spent time visiting classrooms, can confirm it. When I think back on my teachers who were most effective, there is something they all had in common: they all seemed excited to be teaching us. Teachers should always be aware of the attitude and energy they bring into class. I assure you the students are aware of it.

The climate in the classroom makes all the difference. As Ginott (1972) succinctly noted, "Only if a child feels right can he think right." (69) So, how do you foster a great climate in your classroom? Building a strong climate is vitally important, but the good news is: it's really not that hard. Here are three strategies to consider.

Setting the Tone

Teachers have opportunities to set the tone for the class at the beginning of the year as well as at the beginning of each class period. On the first day of school, every student draws conclusions about how the year will be based on their experiences in the classroom on the first day of school. Some students come away optimistic and even excited after the first day; some students come away nervous, anxious, and overwhelmed. What would account for that difference, and what role does the teacher play in this scenario? Did the teacher spend the first day developing the seating chart, going over rules, consequences, expectations, and reviewing the syllabus? Or did the teacher provide opportunities for the class to get to know each other? Did the teacher facilitate "ice breaker" activities, or other fun and engaging experiences for the students? To be sure, there is an appropriate time to go over rules, procedures, and expectations, but the teacher has only one opportunity to create a first impression on the students at the beginning of the year. I remember walking by one classroom on the first day of school and overheard a teacher ask this question to her class: "What would have to happen in here this year for this to be the best class you've ever experienced?" Consider how words like this set the tone in the room. What if each teacher began the year by communicating this sentiment to their students: "You belong in this class. We want you here. Your contributions are valuable. If there is ever a day you're not with us, we will miss you… because you matter."?

By no means, however, does the climate of a classroom hinge entirely on the first day of school. Teachers have the opportunity every day to set the tone in their room. It starts at the door. There are several advantages to teachers standing at the door in between classes. Teachers are able to supervise students and monitor the activity in the hallway. They are able to connect with their colleagues. (I've actually witnessed some powerful collaboration in the minutes that teachers are standing in the hallway.) But perhaps the most important reason for standing at the door is the opportunity it provides teachers to connect with students as they enter their class. I know there have been several teachers who have lit up the internet with their ritual of creative and individualized handshakes with each student who enters the room. That's fun—but not necessary. A genuine smile and a fist bump works just fine. This greeting at the door gives teachers the chance to make a connection and help each student to feel welcome. These brief interactions can also let teachers know when something might not be quite right with a certain student, and they might need to have a follow-up conversation.

I have seen a lot of teachers start class by asking students if they have anything to share. Sure, this reduces some time that the teacher and students can spend on the lesson, but you will learn that time invested in building a good class climate pays big dividends in terms of student engagement with the instructional activities.

Finally, I would note here that teachers set the tone with their attitude and demeanor toward their students. My teenage daughter had talked for several years about how much she loved her fifth-grade teacher. I finally asked her what she liked about her. Her response: "She liked US!" This was simple… yet so profound. Kids gravitate to the teachers that like them. It's important that your students know that you like them. And this knowledge will affect their attitude toward you and toward your class.

Being Vulnerable

As a young teacher, I remember being aggravated with my third-period class because they would not stop talking after I had warned them several times. I raised my voice a bit louder and warned them again. Rashad, who was seated along the wall, continued to talk to the person behind him. I snapped: "Rashad! You have got a thick head! What part of 'be quiet' don't you understand?" The class got quiet, and I don't recall Rashad saying anything for the rest of the class. After a few minutes, I interrupted the class and said something like this: "Y'all, I need to apologize. I lost it. I was frustrated. Rashad, you shouldn't have been talking, but I shouldn't have said that to you; I'm sorry."

It is easy for teachers to assume they need to maintain an air of authority in the classroom. It is tempting for them to think that students should be kept at a distance; professionalism, after all, is paramount. Anything less would undermine the teacher's position and could jeopardize control of the class. This is a common thought process among teachers. Teachers certainly need to maintain their authority in the classroom and, to be sure, "professionalism" is an admirable quality. But part of what students find compelling is when their teachers don't try to hide their own humanity. Teachers make mistakes; they get sick; they get sad; they get nervous; they get frustrated. Students love it when their teachers are "real" with them. They love it when teachers don't take themselves too seriously. There is value in showing some vulnerability in the classroom. It makes teachers genuine; it makes them more personal, and that makes them easier for students to relate to.

When teachers make a mistake, they should acknowledge it. If they wrong a student, they should make it right. Teachers are not perfect, and it always works out best when they do not pretend to be. And here's the thing: the students already know it. They appreciate it when their teachers own up to their mistakes and show a little humility. Vulnerability is not a sign of weakness; it is a sign of strength. And it actually engenders more respect from their students. Furthermore, it creates a climate in the classroom where students are more comfortable being themselves. When the students witness their teachers own their mistakes, it makes them more comfortable taking risks themselves. John Hattie (2012) writes: "An optimal classroom climate for learning is one that generates an atmosphere of trust—a climate in which it is understood that it is okay to make mistakes, because mistakes are the essence of learning." (29)

I would also encourage teachers to be a little silly sometimes. When teachers "let their hair down," it goes a long way to creating a fun environment in the classroom. And this is surely an environment where students are more likely to be engaged. Teachers enjoy their job more when they allow themselves to have a little fun in the classroom. Moreover, it also helps students enjoy the class more too. In *The Seven Habits of Highly Affective Teachers*, Rick Wormeli (2015) puts it this way:

> Having fun with your subject and your students will give students permission to engage, even invest, in their learning, and it will elevate your spirits. There's so much stress involved in teaching today's students; moments of true passion and playfulness bring back much-needed humanity.

Being Aware of your Students

Great teachers always come to class ready to teach, but they are mindful of the fact that not all students come to class ready to learn. They realize all of their students do not walk in the door at the same place—academically, socially, or emotionally. Students come to school with "baggage." The best teachers do not just teach good lessons… they understand the baggage, and they account for this dynamic as they are delivering instruction and as they are interacting with students. Maybe one student was tripped in the hallway by some bigger boys who thought it was funny. He is preoccupied during class thinking about how he can avoid those kids walking to his next class. Another student was up much of the night listening to her parents argue, so she is continually dozing off in class. Another student did not have anyone at home to help him with his homework, so he walks into class feeling embarrassed and behind. As a principal, I remember one sixth-grader who would not go to class because kids had been making fun of his haircut. We need to remember that "Maslow's Hierarchy of Needs" is more than just a theory. We need to be mindful of how the needs of our students might impact the degree to which they will be receptive to the lesson.

Alan Beck (1994) noted, "You can't do the Bloom stuff until you take care of the Maslow stuff." As teachers, we would like to think that our lesson is the most important thing to the student. In reality, everything else in the student's world trumps the lesson. We should always remember that each student walks into our class with a unique set of circumstances—their own struggles and challenges. Effective teachers are sensitive to the needs of their students. They bring empathy, patience, and kindness to their classroom. They create a safe place for students, and this creates a more effective learning environment. When students leave the class feeling better about themselves, their teacher understood that there is more to teaching than delivering instruction. We cannot control the home environment of our students, but we can surely control their classroom environment. When they are under our care, they can feel safe, supported, and loved.

As a young assistant principal, I remember sitting in the back of another math classroom, in awe of the way this teacher handled a potentially embarrassing situation for a student. Students were taking turns working problems at the board. As soon as Malachi got to the board, it was obvious to her that he was not confident in working the problem. With his back to the class, the teacher announced loudly, "So Malachi knows that the first thing he needs to do is write the equation on the board." Malachi proceeded to copy the equation. She then announced: "Malachi knows that he needs to get X by itself, so he is going to subtract six from both sides. And Malachi subtracted six from both sides. And just like that, she walked Malachi through the problem, saving him the humiliation of being stumped at the board. I'm certain I was the only one who knew what was happening. And I marveled at how this teacher masterfully and discretely supported her student.

There is an oft quoted adage: "They may forget what you said, but they will never forget how you made them feel." It is often cited by educators because it so poignantly captures the important role that teachers play in creating a positive climate in their classroom. Good teachers are relentless in encouraging their students. They give out compliments on a regular basis. They avoid sarcasm. They control their own negative emotions. Good teachers work to ensure that their class is an emotionally safe place for all their students because students who feel good about themselves, are in a much better position to actually learn.

I have asked many students over the years what they liked about their teachers. Time and again, they say, "When I have a question, they don't mind explaining it to me." And kids can tell which teachers are patient and which ones are not. It is clear to me that they do not take it for granted when teachers patiently explain and reexplain material. They appreciate classes where they feel comfortable asking questions. I remember striking up a conversation with a young person in the airport about her experiences in school. Her enduring memory related to how her teachers spoke to her—their language, their tone of voice, and their attitude. She acknowledged she was a challenging student, but she recalled vividly how her teachers did not respond to her with patience.

How do we speak to our most challenging students? You might have brilliant lessons… but are you patient with students who need it explained a second or third time? You might utilize all the latest technology… but do you persist with the student who seems to have an attitude? I think these answers matter, but I also believe they reveal much about the professional commitment of teachers. I think teachers shine the most not when they are teaching well-crafted, innovative lessons, but when they are working patiently with students who are struggling. The attitude of the teacher affects the learning environment, and the learning environment always influences what is learned. It is never just about the lesson plan. Noted teacher and child psychologist Haim Ginott (1972) once remarked:

> I've come to a frightening conclusion that I am the decisive element in the classroom. It's my personal approach that creates the climate. It's my daily mood that makes the weather. As a teacher, I possess a tremendous power to make a child's life miserable or joyous. I can be a tool of torture or an instrument of inspiration. I can humiliate or heal. In all situations, it is my response that decides whether a crisis will be escalated or de-escalated and a child humanized or dehumanized.
>
> (13)

Ginott understood that teachers are the most important variable in the classroom. This is a reality every effective teacher understands.

> We all like to be comfortable and all want to feel welcome. My goal is to make my classroom an environment that will do just that. To reach that goal, I decided to be intentional with classroom culture. One way is to implement flexible seating. Kids have the option of sitting on the floor, on a stool, or in a desk. My advice to them is to find somewhere that they feel they learn best. That location may change depending on the student's mood and what we are doing. As a teacher, I have to be okay with that. The benefits have been great in our room. There are few discipline issues, kids are engaged and they take ownership of our room.
>
> Seating is not the only way I am intentional with classroom culture. I want students to feel comfortable sharing and participating. A couple of things that I do to create this type of environment is to greet kids at the door and make an effort to get to know them. I do roll call everyday, which is a fun way to take roll by asking a silly question or something simple about each student. They all have

the option to not answer the question. This allows all of us in the classroom to get to know each other better and makes us more comfortable with each other.

Tracey Carter, Teacher

Organization, instructional techniques, and awareness of student perception are components that helped me solidify a classroom environment conducive to learning. When students entered the classroom, they immediately picked up instructional materials and began the daily bell-ringer. This organization and routine kept students on task and learning at higher levels by immediately engaging in learning activities. I am a firm believer that a classroom environment conducive to learning cannot always be strict business. Students need time and opportunity to build relationships with peers and the teacher. After the bell-ringer, students always had two minutes to talk to friends or share with the whole class something important to them. Intently listening to the students when they shared was important to me. It did not take long to discover if I listened to them, they listened to me. I specifically recall when a 6th grade student came to the board, when asked by me, to solve an equation. She did so well solving the equation with a little help from me. It took some productive struggle, but she did a great job of successfully completing the problem. Later on, I learned that she was humiliated and even embarrassed to walk into the classroom hereafter. How could I have known this? She was smiling and worked so hard to complete the problem. From this experience, I learned that perception is reality for students. When creating a classroom environment conducive to learning, don't forget what students perceive is reality to them.

Daniel Farris, Teacher

As a first-year teacher, I remember being told an age-old piece of "sage" advice: "Don't tell the kids anything personal about yourself." I figured, "Well, they (the advice-givers) have been doing this for a while; they probably know the ropes." Then I went into a classroom of teenaged faces full of hope and wonder and I just couldn't do it. Who wants to be taught by a statue? So now I always tell them who I am, what I stand for, and all about the things I love. No, I don't tell my kids every detail of my life, but they know about my family, where I'm from, that I played volleyball in college, and that I love to work out. In turn, by being vulnerable to them, they feel safe enough to share their most personal stories with me: heartbreak over a divorce or a parent dying, exuberance about that B they finally got in AP US History, and sometimes even the darkest, grittiest things, like that they need money for food or they need help and they knew who to come to. Kids who trust the teacher in their classroom will do a few things, and one of them is to work hard for that teacher. We, as humans, love to make people proud. The other thing they'll do is trust you. And there is no price you can put on that.

Charli Hamlin, Teacher

3

Focusing on the Instruction

Learning to manage your classroom effectively and develop a healthy climate is foundational for meaningful learning. Student teachers quickly discover this truth as they experience that they are, indeed, prerequisites to the essential practice of being a teacher—the actual teaching. So, what is at the heart of being an effective teacher? While there is not one definitive answer here, I know this: being an effective teacher is not fundamentally about being nice, having the right personality, having good relationships with students, having a positive attitude, or even loving the kids. It is about the *learning*! Just to be clear, those other qualities, practices, and dispositions are valuable, and sometimes even critical to the process. (I talk about them at length in this book!) But, ultimately, teaching is about the learning. You can have a great attitude and love the kids, and still not teach an effective lesson. You can have a wonderful personality and a room full of students that love you, but if they are not mastering the objectives in your course of study, you are not being an effective teacher. So, what does it take? That is what we explore in this chapter.

Planning the Lesson

I have never had an affinity for lesson plans. It pains me to say this but, as a new teacher, I remember writing this in my plan book: "Covering chapter 9." That was it. That is what I had written down in my lesson plan book. I remember thinking about what I would do in class that day while I was driving to school. I sort of took pride in my ability to wing it. I also remember my principal admonishing me for my inadequate lesson plans. It was obviously embarrassing to be chastised by my boss, but it also frustrated me. I was frustrated because her focus seemed to be on documentation, and I saw little value in that. I was short-sighted. I am not proud of any of this now, and I don't recommend this approach to teaching.

As I matured as a teacher, I found that I spent more and more time planning. I never liked the necessity or activity of documentation, but I learned to value the process of planning, and I increasingly saw benefit in it. Simply put, well-considered lesson plans can ensure that you are teaching the right curriculum, that you are teaching it in the most effective way possible, and that you are able to verify that students have learned what you hoped they would. I do not think it matters what template, format, or style you use. Your administration might care, however, and you should certainly defer to them. But the plan needs to account for these three things: curriculum, instruction, and assessment.

Thinking about the Curriculum

The first thing to consider is your audience. In *Instructional Planning for Effective Teaching* (2016) Stronge and Xu put it this way: "Teachers must know who students are and whom they are teaching before they can match instruction with students' individual needs." (p. 73) Here are some other questions to consider when thinking about your curriculum:

Are you teaching the required standards mandated by your state and district course of study?

Will the pacing allow you to be at the right point by the end of the quarter, semester, or year?

Are their skills that you hope to embed that may not be explicit in your course of study?

Do your objectives align with your colleagues who are teaching the same course?

Does your curriculum allow you to collaborate with teachers in other disciplines?

What are the essential questions that will drive your instruction?

What is the level of cognitive rigor that will be embedded in the learning.

There is a well-established conceptual framework that is particularly helpful for teachers as they consider the level of thinking that they are planning for their students. Bloom (1956) outlined levels of thinking that represented different levels of cognitive rigor. Bloom's Taxonomy was revised several decades later by Anderson and Krathwohl (2001) and includes the following: Remembering, Understanding, Applying, Analyzing, Evaluating, and Creating. These concepts are useful to teachers as they consider how "deep" they are expecting students to go with the material. Norman Webb (1997) also provided a well-known framework for thinking about assessment and ensuring that it is aligned with expectations. He wrote, "Expectations and assessments are aligned if what is elicited from students on the assessments is as demanding cognitively as what students are expected to know and do." (p. 15) His Depth of Knowledge (DOK) framework ranges from information recall to higher levels of critical thinking. As a young teacher, I was consistently guilty of focusing on the first level of Bloom's Taxonomy: *remembering*. Most of my assessments simply required that students recall copious amounts of information. It is essential that teachers are mindful of the cognitive rigor that they are embedding in their lessons and are intentional about planning for students to think at the higher levels.

Thinking about the Instruction

When teachers are planning for the actual instruction, they should account for the following questions:

What strategies will be most effective for teaching this material?
What learning activities will result in the highest levels of student engagement?
What resources do I need to pull this off?
What will I do about students who finish early?

John Hattie (2009) synthesized the results of thousands of studies about how teachers impact student achievement in his landmark book *Visible Learning*. While there are many instructional strategies and activities that impact student learning, Hattie highlights the ones that research demonstrates to be the most effective. Furthermore, he argues that it is critical that teachers embrace the crucial role they play in making and evaluating instructional decisions for their students.

> There is no recipe, no professional development set of worksheets, no new teaching method, and no band-aid remedy. It is a way of thinking: "My role, as a teacher, is to evaluate the effect I have on my students." It is to "know thy impact", it is to understand this impact, and it is to act on this knowing and understanding.
> (Hattie, 2012, 23)

Another guru of teacher effectiveness, Robert Marzano (2003), also affirmed the crucial role that teachers play: "all researchers agree that the impact of decisions made by individual teachers is far greater than the impact of decisions made at the school level." (71)

Thinking about the Assessment

When planning for assessment, teachers should reflect on these two questions:

What are the various ways that I will be able to gauge student understanding?
What will mastery of the objectives look like and what is the best tool to assess that?

Dufour, Dufour, Eaker, and Many (2010) described four essential questions that teachers should consider when thinking about student outcomes. Although they write about these questions in the context of their work on *Professional Learning Communities*, they are still a useful way for teachers to frame their planning for assessments. For them, the planning process comes down to these four questions:

> *What do I want students to know and be able to do?*
> *How will I know when they know it and can do it?*
> *What will I do if they don't know it or can't do it?*
> *What will I do with the students who already know it or can do it?*

These are important questions, and they deserve to be answered by the teacher as they are planning for a lesson or unit. Writing lesson plans is not fun for most teachers, and I'm not a big fan of strict documentation following prescribed formats. But the process of planning your lessons is vitally important. Please do not shortchange this component.

Teaching the Students

Instruction is the core business of educators. Not much else matters if teachers are not solid in this capacity. The research of Hattie confirms that there is no single instructional strategy that teachers need to employ but, rather, there is a wide variety of research proven practices and activities that teachers can utilize to enhance student learning. Effective teaching can take many forms and can reflect the different styles and personalities of teachers. My intention here is not to prescribe how teachers should do their job, but to highlight several facets to instruction that teachers ought to consider.

Engagement

I remember being bored a lot in school. I remember watching the minutes on the clock tick by, just waiting on the bell to ring. I remember writing silly poems in class, just to pass the time. I remember seeing how long I could hold my breath. I remember repeatedly starting and stopping my digital watch, trying to stop it with the tenth and hundredth seconds reading all zeros. And of course I remember sleeping. I'm sure many of you have some similar memories that you could recall from your time in school. Far too many students have far too many experiences of being disengaged in a classroom. Actually, as a young teacher, I remember my principal doing an observation in my class and making a note on my evaluation that "four students had their heads on their desk." Clearly, my students were not always engaged! As educators we need to remember that while we can compel student attendance, their learning is always voluntary. So, what's the secret to student engagement?

There isn't one! There is no magic strategy, there is no surefire activity, and there certainly is no formula. My point in writing this is simply to get you to account for this in your planning and to offer some thoughts to inspire your thinking.

There was a sign in my dentist's office that read, "You don't have to floss all your teeth—just the ones you want to keep." I have thought about making a sign for my office that reads, "Teachers don't have to care about all their lessons—just the lessons they want their students to learn." What students find most compelling in a classroom is usually not the brilliantly scaffolded lesson, and it's certainly not the dry textbook; it's the energy, attitude, and enthusiasm of the teacher. Students are not typically motivated by lessons as much as they are motivated by teachers. My oldest son never liked English. He did not like to read, and he did not like to write. But, in the tenth grade, his favorite class was English. Why? He came home on a regular basis talking about how passionate his teacher was. The teacher's enthusiasm and excitement for the lessons created an interest in the subject for my son. These experiences reinforced for me that the energy teachers bring to their lesson has a profound impact on the extent to which students are engaged in the lesson. They remind me that student engagement is usually in direct proportion to teacher enthusiasm.

My most memorable teacher—the one who motivated me the most—was Mr. Navarre. He taught me Earth Science when I was in the eighth grade, and that was the year I learned to love rocks. I loved rocks because Mr. Navarre loved rocks. His passion and energy for the subject inspired me to care about the subject. As teachers, it is unreasonable for us to expect students to engage in our lesson when we are not that excited about teaching it. But, on the flip side, genuine enthusiasm from the teacher can make almost any lesson engaging. I still own the rock box that I constructed in Mr. Navarre's class. It sits on my shelf as a constant reminder of that powerful truth.

Author and publisher Dave Burgess (2012) has traveled the country inspiring educators to "Teach Like a Pirate." He challenges teachers to create exciting and dynamic lessons that are so compelling students would come to your class even if they didn't have to. He writes that every teacher has the energy and creativity to be that special teacher if they are just willing to tap into it—challenging teachers to "intentionally find ways to bring passion to our work every day." (4)

Phillip Schlechty (2002, 2011) has also written about engaging instruction, but his work has focused on the quality of work that teachers ask students to do, not necessarily the quality of the teacher's performance. His work is predicated in part, on the assumption that "teachers are leaders and inventors, and students are volunteers. What students have to volunteer is their attention and commitment." (xvii) He describes the ten design qualities that define engaging work, and suggests that the primary job of teachers is to design work that has these qualities:

- ◆ Content and Substance: What are the students going to learn? What are the standards/guidelines to which the curriculum aligns and the level of student interest?
- ◆ Organization of Knowledge: The way work is organized, planning pacing
- ◆ Clear and Compelling Product Standards: Can students speak to what they are doing?
- ◆ Protection from Adverse Consequences: Students feel safe and secure to take risks
- ◆ Product Focus: Student-created product, exhibition, or performance
- ◆ Affirmation: Work is visible to others
- ◆ Affiliation: Students work in teams

- ◆ Novelty and Variety: Something new, providing a variety of media and resources
- ◆ Choice: Students have options and choices about how they work, how they learn
- ◆ Authenticity: Is the work authentically interesting to the student?

Schlechty argues that student engagement is a function of the extent to which teachers design work for them that reflects these qualities.

Differentiation

Much has been written about the different learning styles of students, and this is for good reason. Kids learn differently. Some students learn best by seeing, some learn best by hearing, some learn best by doing and exploring. Certainly, the goal of every teacher should be the success of each student. As teachers, we want to teach lessons in ways that create the best opportunity for our students to process and understand the material. That means we should design lessons that address all the different learning styles. Carol Tomlinson (2017), who has written extensively about differentiated instruction, has described it as being a proactive approach to student learning, focused on quality of work rather than quantity of work, connected to regular formative assessment, evidenced in multiple approaches to the lesson, student centered, and reflected in a combination of whole group, small group, and individualized instruction. When asked in an interview (Rebora, 2008) about how she recognized differentiated instruction in a classroom, her response underscored the significance of teachers focusing on the needs of their students:

> One of the first things I look for are teacher–student connections. Does this seem to be a teacher who is really paying attention to the kids, who's going out of his or her way to study them and understand what makes them tick? To be effective with differentiation, a teacher really needs to talk with the kids, ask them their opinions on things, sit down with them for a minute or two to see how

things are going, and listen to them and find out what they are interested in. All that feeds back into instruction. And teacher–student connections not only help teachers plan what to do with kids, it also provides motivation for differentiation: If I can see kids as real individual human beings, I'm going to be much more invested in helping them learn and grow individually.

Differentiated instruction is not the goal, but it *is* an inevitable result when teachers are committed to the success of every student.

The Four Cs

Regardless of your discipline, it is important to be mindful that there are skills that transcend your prescribed course of study. One particularly poignant set of skills is outlined in a document developed by the National Education Association (NEA): "Preparing 21st Century Students for a Global Society: An Educator's Guide to the 'Four Cs'". The skills are Critical Thinking, Communication, Collaboration, and Creativity.

Critical Thinking

This umbrella term refers to the skills of reasoning, analyzing, synthesizing, interpreting, and reflecting. (8–9)

Communication

This involves articulating ideas effectively and listening for understanding. It also includes the ability to communicate in a variety of contexts and with different technologies. (14)

Collaboration

Collaboration is described as the ability to work with others, be flexible in groups, and share responsibility as part of a team. (20)

Creativity

This refers to the ability to develop new ideas and implement innovative concepts or strategies. (25)

The challenge for teachers is to explore ways to integrate these skills into their instruction and incorporate activities that foster their development. This document by the NEA provides a variety of examples of how this can be accomplished in typical classrooms and includes a wealth of further resources to assist teachers in this endeavor.

Busywork

This section is included as a warning. Please do not give busywork. I suspect every teacher has been guilty of this at one time or another. I know I have. But it is a practice to avoid. Most students know when the work they are given does not have much value; they recognize when the assignment is intended primarily to keep them busy and quiet. Busywork can have the effect of making students cynical about school, and it can undermine respect for the teacher and the class. So, please do everything possible to plan activities and assignments for students that are worthwhile. You only have a limited amount of time with your students each day. Try to make the minutes count.

Technology

Chances are, younger teachers have an easier time integrating technology into their classroom. Many of them might not remember a time without smart phones and the internet. They are part of the generation that has come to be known as "digital natives," a term coined by Mark Prenski (2001). Many veteran teachers have struggles with learning and implementing new technologies because it is so far out of their comfort zone. The point I want to make here is that the interest of comfort level of the teacher should not be the ultimate criteria for whether or not a certain strategy or technology is utilized in the classroom. Ultimately, what should drive every teacher when they are planning a lesson is this question: What is the most effective way to teach this objective? Or, better still: What is the best way to ensure the students learn what they need to learn?

Teachers should always remember that technology is a tool; it is not a gimmick or a fad. And technology is certainly not the end in and of itself. Computers, smart phones, interactive white boards, and apps—these are all wonderful innovations that allow teachers to do their job more efficiently, engage students more effectively, and differentiate their assignments in a way that increases their effectiveness. It is also important to remember that advances in technology will continue. Former National Secretary of Education, Richard Riley, is reported to have said, "We are currently preparing students for jobs that don't yet exist … using technologies that haven't been invented … in order to solve problems we don't even know are problems yet." There is no way that teachers can effectively prepare students for their future if they do not continue to integrate modern technologies into their classrooms.

Equity

Much has been written about achievement gaps over the last several decades and, in recent years, significant work has been done around the concept of equity. This is for good reason. Most school mission statements pay lip service to the idea. For example, you see phrases such as "educating every child" or "helping each student reach their own unique potential." But, year after year, decade after decade, students of color and students in poverty continue to be left behind. With the more recent focus on disparate learning outcomes among students, there is also a new way that educators are framing the challenge. Theresa Mooney, writing for the *Teach for America Organization* notes: "Simply stated, we believe the term 'achievement gap' unfairly places blame on kids. It implies that children are not achieving as they should be, and that it's their fault." She argues that the societal barriers are the biggest threat to equity, so she makes the case that it is more accurate to refer to an "opportunity gap" (2018). Paul Gorski poignantly discusses this challenge and offers hope to teachers in his important book, *Reaching and Teaching Students in Poverty: Strategies for Erasing the Opportunity Gap* (2018). While students are confronted with a variety of barriers outside of school, Gorski challenges teachers to be part of the solution: "We have the power and, of course, the responsibility to ensure we do not reproduce inequitable conditions in our own classrooms and schools." (3)

Building on the ground breaking work of Ladson-Billings (1994) and Geneva Gay (2000), other authors have written about the imperative of "culturally responsive teaching" (Gay, 2000). In 2020, New America released a reflection guide for teachers to guide their efforts in providing a culturally responsive classroom. It included eight competencies:

1) Reflect on one's cultural lens
2) Recognize and redress bias in the system
3) Draw on student's culture to share curriculum and instruction
4) Bring real-world issues into the classroom
5) Model high expectations for all students
6) Promote respect for student differences
7) Collaborate with families and the local community
8) Communicate in linguistically and culturally responsive ways.

Effective teachers need to be effective for *every* student. This means they recognize not every student learns the same, and not every student has the same challenges or opportunities. They work to capitalize on the unique strengths of their students and strive to mitigate their challenges.

Assessing the Learning

Assessment is not actually separate from the instructional process; it is an important part of it. It does not just measure student learning; it drives it. Educators often differentiate between *formal* and *informal* assessments. Informal assessments are often spontaneous and not usually documented. They might include discussion between teacher and student, or anecdotal observations that teachers make as they interact with students and move around the class. It involves the ongoing professional judgment of teachers as they gauge the extent to which students are mastering the lesson objectives. Formal assessments are what most teachers typically think of when someone mentions assessments. These are planned ahead of time and typically structured. These could include quizzes, tests, or projects.

It can also be helpful to differentiate between formative assessment and summative assessment. Summative assessments are usually done at the end of a unit, and they serve the purpose of providing a grade for your gradebook. Formative assessments are done during the unit rather than at the end, and they provide teachers with feedback on how their instruction needs to be modified and how students need to be supported. So, while summative assessments measure and record the learning, formative assessments actually impact the student learning. And while it is easy for teachers to be preoccupied with the formal and summative assessment found in numeric or letter grades, the most effective teachers are more concerned with formative assessments. Tomlinson and McTighe (2006) talk about the function of grading this way: "We believe that the primary goal of grading and reporting is to *communicate to important audiences, such as students and parents, high-quality feedback to support the learning process and encourage learner success.*" (129) It is worth noting here that their explanation underscores the role that assessments play in facilitating the learning process. Rick Wormeli (2006) explains that the three main reasons we grade are to provide feedback, document progress, and inform instructional decisions. He passionately argues that the feedback that comes through formative assessment is the most important part of the assessment process: "Real learning of both the topic and personal responsibility comes from specific, timely, and frequent feedback to students during the learning, not after the learning." (24)

I remember a teacher who would always pester me about when the state test results were coming in. She could not wait to see how her students did. She spent countless hours tutoring her students and would do anything to help them succeed. She saw the success of her students as a reflection of the work she had done. It has been said, "Until something is learned, nothing is taught." That's a tough adage, but great teachers are willing to own it.

Several years ago, I remember walking into Mr. Farris's room during his planning period. He was finishing grading tests. He looked a little dejected as he remarked to me: "These students all did poorly. Somehow, I didn't communicate the material as well as I thought I had. I'm gonna reteach it and then assess them again." It can be hard for teachers to swallow their pride in those circumstances, but that is what good teachers are willing to do. They understand the bottom line is always student learning, and ensuring student success is what motivates them. Good teaching is not just about delivering lessons; it is about being invested in the success of your students. That teacher who could not wait for the scores to come in was not actually "pestering" me. I loved her passion. I loved her commitment. I loved the fact that she was invested in the success of her students. It is great when teachers define their success by the success of their students—when they understand it is not about the teaching; it's about the learning.

Finding time to prepare for a class that is a new one for you can be challenging. Do not be afraid to ask a colleague for advice about ways to present lessons that you feel uncomfortable with. Many textbooks include a lot of planning ideas, but some subjects seem to require more preparation than others. As a math teacher, I always had lots of examples ready when introducing a new topic. I would work each example out ahead of time. I found that if I just used made up a problem during class, it would often contain a skill that was not part of the lesson. This bad example would lead to frustration and wasted time. Therefore, I learned to have examples written down in order from easy to more complex. Also, as I presented each problem, I would look into the eyes of my students. I cannot stress enough the value of eye contact. I was able to sense whether I needed to re-explain a particular problem or step, or if I needed to leave out some examples. Not only can understanding, frustration, lack of focus, confusion, and boredom be seen in a student's eyes; but eye contact helps to create a teacher/student bond. It's not a good idea to teach to the board or back wall.

Cynthia Cirone, Teacher

Instruction cannot be separated from the person of the teacher. To teach is to share one's self with a classroom of students. Take my English class. An English lesson is not just a lesson—it is part of who I am. To critique my teaching is to critique something fundamental about who I am. I do not think many accountants weave some aspect of their soul into your tax returns, but ask teachers about lessons they are both proud of and passionate about, and you will see deep into them as people. You will see how they view the world, how they view their students, how they view themselves. At times, I am the guide on the side, and other times I am the sage on the stage; however, I am always me in my classroom. How can I motivate, persuade, and initiate student-centered learning if they are disinterested, disconnected, and disempowered with the content material? To interest, connect, and empower students in English or any content area, I must, at the start, be its conduit. And to be a conduit, I must connect myself to the content and the instruction.

Michael Sinnott, Teacher

In terms of instruction, I believe that it is very important to be transparent and present with students in terms of the learning material. When I first went to college, I realized that I had never been strategically taught to write a paper, and I had to learn the process on my own. Today's students are the same—they need to be systematically taught to write. Part of making each assignment both important and beneficial is putting aside insecurities and allowing students to see the process. It is important for students to know that the teacher is willing to complete all assignments alongside them. When the teacher also completes the assignment, it demonstrates a commitment to the objective and increases the value of the learning opportunity. When I assign students a writing activity, I model the process to them explaining that I, too, make mistakes and corrections. This gives the kids a chance to ask specific questions as well as to see an example of what I am looking for. I know that many young teachers are self-conscious about this type of modeling, but in terms of instruction, it is one of the most valuable ways to both reach students and display the importance of an assignment. It is unnerving at first, but allowing oneself to be corrected by students during the writing process helps students learn while also building a safe learning environment where students are comfortable taking risks and seeking feedback.

Crystal Lamar, Teacher

4

Making the Professional Commitment

My knee had been bothering me for several months, so I finally broke down and went to my orthopedist. He ordered an X-ray, but that did not reveal anything. He checked my mobility and strength in his examining room, but that did not reveal anything either. So he ordered an MRI. I met with him a few days later and got my results. "That cloudy area you see in the image is an edema on your femur," the doctor reported. "A what?" He said, "It's a bone bruise." My doctor said it was comparable to a stress fracture. I had to be on a crutch for six weeks, and I couldn't run for three months! As I was feeling sorry for myself, it occurred to me that my experience served as a model for education.

Physicians, like many professionals, are compelled to improve their practice because their livelihood depends on it. They utilize the latest research, the latest medicine, and the latest technology. Their practice will not survive without this commitment. Imagine a scenario where my doctor says, "Well... the X-ray didn't reveal any breaks, so I don't know what to tell you. I guess you should rest your knee and put some ice on it." Or... "I realize that some orthopedists use MRIs, but my office staff doesn't feel comfortable with that type of technology." These scenarios are obviously absurd. We take for granted that our doctors will be relentless in identifying our injury or illness, and will use whatever technology, medicine, or therapy, is available to "fix" us.

Educators do not really have the same built-in accountability that many other professionals have. The students will keep showing up in our classes whether we are following "best practices" or not. Students cannot typically "shop around" for the teachers with the most research based instructional strategies. They cannot pick and choose their teachers based on which ones capitalize on the most innovative technology and utilize the most authentic assessments. But every school in America has teachers who approach their profession with the same commitment that drives my orthopedist. They treat their students as individuals that have unique needs and talents. They experiment with different instructional strategies to see which ones are the most effective. They steal ideas and activities from colleagues that will enhance their classroom. They embrace the challenge of refining their "desk-side manner" so that all of their students feel valued and respected. They commit themselves to learning new technologies that will allow them to teach and assess students more effectively. In this chapter, we will examine the role that personal professional growth can play for teachers.

In the summer of 2015, I had been researching math proficiency scores for schools all around our state when I was confronted with some data that I never expected. (We were competitive with our test scores, and I wanted to know where we ranked, relative to other schools around the state.) For most grades, the same predictable schools led the way, and the top few spots were always dominated by the usual high achievers. These were schools in affluent school districts, whose students had every advantage imaginable when taking standardized tests. But that year, I noticed there was a small, somewhat obscure school whose fourth-grade math scores were tied for number one in the entire state. And this school had almost 40 percent of their student population served by free or reduced lunch. This was an anomaly that piqued my attention! In a small school, the test scores can often rest on the shoulders of just one or two teachers in each grade. I had to find out who this fourth-grade math teacher was. This teacher was not just beating the odds—she was destroying them. So, that summer, I sent an email to the principal. I introduced myself; I congratulated him on the academic achievements of his students (especially his fourth-grade math students!) and I asked if I could come for a visit. The principal responded graciously and welcomed a visit. So, I took a two-hour road trip to uncover the "magic" behind these phenomenal results. I remember sitting in that principal's office and asking him what was going on in fourth-grade math. He said, "I've got two teachers. One of them is really good, and the other one is off the charts amazing." So I asked him, "Tell me about the one who is off the charts amazing. What makes her so awesome?" He paused, was quiet, and did not seem to have a response. He seemed caught off guard by my question, as if he had never considered the qualities that defined his teacher. Finally, he said: "She's just relentless. She'll do anything to help a student understand math. She'll try any strategy. She'll find any resource. She'll do whatever it takes for her students to be successful." That was it. It was not about the right program. It was not about the newest technology. And there was no magic. It was a teacher who defined her success by the success of her students. It was a teacher who was willing to do whatever it took for her students to learn—for her students to thrive. That was several years ago, but I am still inspired thinking about that teacher.

Recall the story of Mr. Farris from Chapter 3—the teacher who was frustrated with the low grades. This is a teacher who wanted to get better. He wanted it for his students. Most excellent teachers did not start out that way, but they were committed to refining their craft. Every teacher can be a better teacher, and this commitment is what separates the good ones from the great ones. These are four strategies I recommend teachers embrace in their professional journey: take ownership, reflect, be willing to fail, and collaborate.

Take Ownership

This first one is not so much a strategy as it is a mindset. There is a certain amount of professional growth that is bound to occur with any teacher, simply as a function of experience. But the thing is, teachers should be improving intentionally, not accidentally. As Ginott (1972: 63) wrote, "Improvement seldom occurs spontaneously. More often it is attained by deliberate effort." Many schools will have professional learning goals or professional development initiatives that dictate the professional learning in which teachers engage. That's not necessarily a bad thing, but teachers should not limit themselves to that.

As a teacher, what are you curious about? What are you interested in? What do you view as a relative weakness? What are the gaps in your own practice that you should target? When teachers look for ways to foster their own professional interests, when they pursue new knowledge and skills that they are passionate about, they will be emotionally invested in the process and will find the end result more meaningful. This type of personalized professional learning can significantly enhance a teacher's level of professional satisfaction. Teachers who are actively pursuing their passions are fulfilled in a way that those who are merely sticking with the status quo are not. Moreover, teachers who feel they are in control of their own professional learning are inherently more engaged in the process.

Reflect

When a lesson does not go as planned, great teachers are not looking around at the students; they are looking in the mirror. Every teacher experiences lessons that bomb. Effective teachers do not view these lessons as complete failures though, because they learn from them. They do not blame the students; in fact, they are not looking to blame anyone. Instead, they are reflecting on their own role in the process. They are thinking about how the objective might have been stated more clearly; they are thinking about a more strategic way to group the students; they are thinking about what activity might have made the topic seem more relevant; they are thinking about how a different assessment at the end of class might have brought more effective closure to the lesson. Effective teachers understand their pivotal role in the success of every lesson, and they are continually reflecting on their own practice in order to improve. Jim Knight (2011) talked about it this way: "looking back, looking at, and looking ahead." (37) John Hattie (2012) describes the impact of reflective teachers this way: "It is critical that teachers learn about the success or otherwise of their interventions: those teachers who are students of their own impact are the teachers who are the most influential in raising students' achievement." (20) Consider how the following reflective questions might lead to more effective teaching and learning:

I wonder what would make this lesson more interesting for the students.

I wonder if the activity would be more effective if they worked in groups.

I wonder if it will make a difference if I assign the groups differently.

I wonder why those students seem reluctant to participate.

I wonder why everyone missed that question on the test.

I wonder if there is a way to connect this lesson to something they already know.

If the students ask me, "Why do we need to know this stuff?," will I have a good answer for them?

What content knowledge in this unit is really important to me?

What are the skills that I want the students to master in this lesson?

How are my colleagues teaching this lesson? I wonder if their way is more effective.

What is going to be the best way to assess student understanding?

Is there a way to give students choice in how they will learn the material and how they will be assessed on it?

What would motivate my students to care about this lesson?

Would changing the arrangement of desks in my room create a more effective environment for learning?

Would I want to participate in this lesson if I were a student?

It is also beneficial to recruit your students to engage in the process of "reflecting." I have witnessed many teachers give surveys to their students to great effect. It is a good idea to give these surveys to the students in the middle of the year and at the end of the year. You can obviously tweak the questions to fit your grade level, but ask students what they like about the class; what they don't like; what activities have been the most enjoyable; what activities seemed like a waste of time; what do they need more support in; what can be done to improve their experience in the class. Students are usually more candid when you allow them to be anonymous, so that is what I recommend. (I will note that the feedback will be more authentic, more meaningful, and less hurtful if you have done some of the things outlined in Chapter 2 and you have built a healthy class climate.)

Be Willing to Fail

I still remember sitting in Ms. Skellie's class and hearing her tell her students, "I'm nervous about this lesson. I've never done anything like this before." I remember how proud I was of her at that moment. Rarely do I get more excited than when teachers tell me they are trying something new in their classroom. And sometimes they say, "That part didn't work in first period, but I'll tweak it for the rest of my classes." It inspires me when teachers push through some discomfort, when they take risks, and when they learn through their failures. Teachers who choose to remain comfortable in their classroom will probably not make many mistakes. But they will probably never be innovative either; and they will certainly never reach their potential as educators. Professional growth requires a measure of vulnerability, so teachers who are serious about improving their craft need to be willing to occasionally step out on that limb.

Collaborate

When I interview teachers, I usually spend some time talking about the culture of our school. And I often say something like this to the applicant:

> One of our non-negotiables is collaboration. When the adults work together, students benefit. So, if you're the

kind of teacher that likes to just close their door and do your own thing, you're probably not a good fit with our school.

In my experience, there is little that can do more to strengthen the culture of a school and improve the practice of educators than when teachers collaborate with one another. Here are four approaches to learning from colleagues: attend workshops and conferences, participate in professional learning communities, observe peers, and leverage social media.

Attend Workshops and Conferences

Don't be shy about asking your administration for funds to attend training outside your building. While these sessions provide the opportunity to learn from great speakers and presenters, these trainings also provide a valuable context for networking—a chance to forge new professional relationships, expose yourself to new ideas, new attitudes, and new approaches to your craft. Many teachers that I've spoken to report that the informal networking that takes place at conferences is the most valuable part of the experience. In addition to the professional growth that is generated, teachers are able to cultivate genuine connections with peers, and this camaraderie can go a long way toward sustaining them in those seasons when the profession may become a grind.

Participate in Professional Learning Communities

Dufour, Dufour, Eaker, and Many (2010) define professional learning communities (PLCs) as an "ongoing process in which educators work collaboratively in recurring cycles of collective inquiry and action research to achieve better results for the students they serve." (11) While they maintain that PLCs should be understood as an entire school or district, the essential work is done in collaborative teams within the school. These are simply groups of professional educators who collaborate to improve student learning. According to DuFour (2004), PLCs are organized around three "big ideas": they are singularly focused on student learning; they are driven by a genuine commitment to collaboration; and they are relentlessly committed to achieving results. PLCs can be made up of teachers who share the same students, like the teams that are common in middle schools. They could be a group of elementary teachers who teach the same grade or maybe some high school teachers who share the same subject. In PLCs, teachers collaborate on learning objectives, instructional activities, development of common assessments, and analyzing of data. They can be a wonderful opportunity for teachers to lean on each other and learn from one another. As a principal, I have witnessed firsthand the powerful role that PLCs have played with our teachers. They have provided opportunities to plan lessons together, share activities, reflect on assessments, not to mention the support and camaraderie that is typically found in these meetings.

Observe Peers

Teachers need their breaks, and their planning time is precious. I get it. But do not underestimate the value of observing another teacher in their classroom, even if it's just for five minutes. When you observe a colleague, you are exposed to new instructional strategies; you learn the value of different routines and procedures; and you may notice a new way to handle challenging student behavior. This type of professional learning is not theoritical; it is as practical as it gets. Sometimes, teachers sit in a conference or workshop and listen to an "expert" talk about what teachers need to be doing, and they think to themselves: "That sounds good, but you don't know my students." Or, "You don't understand the challenges in our school." When you are observing your colleague, you can be assured they are working in the same world as you. They are not pontificating to well-behaved adults; they are in the trenches, doing the same work as you. There certainly is value to professional learning outside of your building, but never underestimate the value of learning from the expert down the hall.

Leverage Social Media

Whitaker, Zoul, and Casas (2015) talk about the value of professional learning networks (PLNs) in *What Connected Educators Do*

Differently. Being connected to other teachers on social media can challenge you and inspire you. Through cultivating a PLN, teachers can tap into a wealth of knowledge and expertise that can open all sort of doors for professional growth opportunities.

I recently reached out to my PLN on Twitter, asking what my fellow educators did to improve their own level of effectiveness as an educator. Here are some of the responses:

Reflection! Take 10 minutes every day to reflect on your lessons and make notes of what did and didn't work, plus what could you do next time. Review this in the summer, or in the lead up to the next time you plan to teach those lesson.

Dave Dunsavage (@MrDunsavage)

All year long I keep a list of things that didn't go well, or ideas to implement for next year. I just jot things down as they come up and at the beginning of each new year I revisit it and put those things into effect.

Rahkola Cox (@MsRahkola)

I ask for help or ideas from lots of different teachers, my counselor, instructional coaches, admin. 17 years in and I'm still soaking up knowledge from my peers.

Angela Proske (@MrsAProske)

Watching other teachers teach. We so rarely get to do this but it is so motivating and powerful!

Kathleen Décosse (@decosse_k)

Experiment. Try new ways of teaching the same stuff. And I keep a daily log of what I did. I make notes of what works.

Jess Meade (@docjessm)

I ask the students how their consumer experience is and ask pointed questions for meaningful feedback.

Samantha Wasson (@SamanthaWasson_)

Video of myself teaching…set goal…implement…reflect.
Jacquelyn Kennedy (@jackenn27)

Spend more time planning. Think through lines of questioning to get to deeper levels of thinking. Put a timer on your lesson. Where are you spending the most time? Video yourself and do self assessment. Have a mentor assess your video and lesson.
David Friedli (@FriedYo)

Conferences—not just the presentations but talking to other teachers in between sessions and trading ideas.
(@annmariastat)

Reflection, reading books or watching videos by others I admire, and do surveys of students and parents.
Jocelyn Logan (@jalogan76)

Take the time to watch & learn from the classroom experts in my building & in our district! How they build relationships with students we may share, teaching style, & the authentic joy they have for education. There's nothing better.
Mitchell Pittman (@QBCoachP)

Reflect on what works and what doesn't work. Learn to use new technology. Read. Share experiences with colleagues who have similar teaching style. Always be open to learning something new.
Jennifer Taylor (@TaylorTaylorjen)

I'd audio or video record myself in class and think would I like to be in my class based on what I saw/heard.
Steve Nendza (steve_nendza)

Working towards and attaining National Board Certification. Nothing else has had a more profound impact on my growth as a teacher. 100%.
(@mrscaieOHS)

Learning new tech is helpful. Reflecting on lessons daily; giving surveys to students to find out if what you're doing is working & asking them for their input on how to make things better if necessary; including Ssin decisions, rubric creation & learning pathways.

Jenn Vedder (@CoachVedder_HPE)

Ask sts about learning needs and input on the class. Read/Listen to podcasts/research. Apply new strategies. Evaluate. Reflect with students.

Fabiola Vacatoledo (@SpanishTesorito)

Surrounding yourself with people who are like-minded in growth of their craft. People feed off the excitement of others. Twitter has been a wonderful example of this.

Sandy Batherson (@sandybatherson)

My greatest growth comes from something that we rarely get the opportunity to do: watch other teachers teach. Not Professional development or seminars, but actually watch other teachers in their class. Subject doesn't matter. I'm looking for styles, procedures & relationships.

John Mulvaney (@johnKmulvaney)

For me it's communicating with the students. Asking them directly what works and what does not. I establish a trusting relationship from the get-go. And also knowing their needs individually, so I can better address them.

Katia Lévy (@Frenchbiche)

I consistently ask the students what's working and what's not. I ask them for suggestions and for honest feedback. I've done that every quarter, every year I've taught.

Theresa Poquis (@TPoquis)

Collaboration with other educators, reflection, and feedback. Actively seeking ideas and continually trying new things. PLNs. Learning about my students and from them. Being ok with not getting it right the first time.

Meaghan Hegarty (@MegHegarty)

Observing other teachers and having them observe you.

Rebekah Hebert (@reb2911)

Reflect daily about what went well and what I would do differently, teaching or interaction with students and colleagues. Reach out to colleagues and students to get feedback, ask questions and get ideas. Think process not task completion.

Sherrill Hudson (@SherrillHudson1)

Of the more than two hundred responses I received from teachers, these were the dominant themes that emerged concerning how teachers who feel like them improve in their practice:

♦ Collaborate with and observe colleagues
♦ Solicit feedback from students
♦ Reflect on what worked and what didn't

While this feedback is anecdotal, it is entirely consistent with what I have observed as a school administrator for almost 20 years.

The professional commitment of teachers to honing their craft is not merely a clinical ambition, however; it is rooted in their mission as educators. Effective teachers are not motivated to improve for their own satisfaction; they want to be better for their students. In his best-selling book *What Great Teachers Do Differently*, Todd Whitaker (2020) writes, "Great teachers have high expectations for students but even higher expectations for themselves." (48) The most effective teachers hold themselves to a high standard, and they demonstrate a tireless commitment to being better tomorrow than they were today.

As a teacher and life-long learner, I have always wanted to know more. People I have met assume that because I have a PhD in biochemistry, that I am super smart and "know everything". Not so. In my PhD I learned a lot about a very specific slice of biochemistry, and importantly, I was very persistent. Along the way I learned that the more research I did, the less I knew. There were always more interesting questions waiting to side track you. And in research as connections between ideas were revealed, they also raised more questions. So how do you stay afloat in this ever deepening pool of questions? Focus on what you have decided is important in your curriculum.

As a PhD scientist turned AP chemistry teacher, I focused on developing a strong lab program. From my own research, I knew specific lab techniques would be useful in college and in a science career. I made sure to connect each technique to the data it produced and linked the data analysis to the conclusions that could be drawn. I strengthened my lab program through participation in high quality professional development: Advanced Placement Summer Institutes in chemistry and chemistry education specific conferences such as ChemEd and American Chemical Society workshops at NSTA conventions.

Katie Scheirer, Teacher

The way I approach professional growth and development is to acquire new experiences. The simplest paths to development are usually in or close to my own classroom. I try several new lessons each unit, sometimes I have to retreat back to what is comfortable, but most of the time I can make small changes to make the lesson very meaningful. Taking the time to purposefully reflect on my lessons usually allows me to transform even the most spectacular failures into great learning experiences, for me and future students, but that would be impossible if I did not try something new to begin with. When my coworkers and I have a commonly planned lesson I also listen to their successes and failures to help modify my own lessons.

During my planning period I visit a classroom of a different subject at least once a month. I often find that other disciplines solve problems and manage their classrooms in different, quite unique ways compared to my own or those I normally observe from similar minds.

I try to attend at least two professional development conferences within my own teaching discipline each year. I like to attend them alone if it is the first time for a given conference so I am more likely to meet new people and hear their perspective on delivering specific content. Even when I repeat attendance of an annual conference, I find that I usually gain more from the breakout sessions since they typically differ, and I usually attend with a peer so we can compare ideas.

Josh Elliot, Teacher

Teacher collaboration is when teachers work together towards achieving a common goal of increasing student learning by sharing their ideas and working together. Collaboration is important because it helps to develop better lesson planning with more rigor involved. When teachers collaborate about the planning of their lessons, they are able to create better lessons that will show results of work that challenges students' thinking in new and interesting ways. I've learned that when I collaborate with my coworkers, our great minds go to work. We are able to create some of the best lessons from bouncing ideas off of each other. I've also found that collaboration helps to create an environment for all teachers to share in the responsibility for all students' learning. What I mean by this, is that we are responsible for all kids succeeding. We have to look beyond our own classes and learn to celebrate each other as a team and the success of all students.

Trust and relationships also develop from collaboration among colleagues. When you work as a team, you understand that it's okay to admit what worked for you and what didn't work. You have to know that collaboration is needed because it helps to bring out the best in you. In other words, you have to be honest and transparent with yourself. It's okay to admit that a lesson didn't go so well and to ask for ideas from your coworkers that may have had more success teaching a lesson than you. I love getting feedback from my colleagues about their successes and failures in teaching a lesson. It shows me that we are all in this together and no one is perfect, not even teachers.

Lakesha Fleming, Teacher

Part II

The Second Dimension

The Relational Perspective

5

Remembering Your Purpose

"People don't buy WHAT you do, they buy WHY you do it." (42) This familiar quote from Simon Sinek (2011) speaks to the power of knowing your purpose. In his popular book *Start With Why*, Sinek builds on the concept of "The Golden Circle" to explain the pattern of communicating human behavior. The Golden Circle is an image of three circles—a smaller circle, an outside circle, and a middle circle.

He argues that most companies communicate to their customers by explaining *what* they do, *how* they do it, and then *why* they do it in that order. The premise of his book, however, is that the most successful companies communicate from the inside out. The companies who "start with why" inspire the greatest loyalty because they remain grounded in their core values. This approach makes an emotional connection with customers, resonating with them on a visceral level. Put another way, he says that companies should try to win the hearts of customers before they try to win their minds. Although Sinek's book is predicated on a corporate model, I think it also can be applied to education. Consider the Golden Circle of teachers:

The outside circle—the WHAT of our profession might be: *Teaching Third Grade Language Arts*

The middle circle—the HOW might be: *Using research based and pedagogically sound instructional strategies and activities*

The inner circle—the WHY might be: *Making a difference in the life of a child… or Giving students hope… or Creating a brighter future for the next generation*

Just as Sinek makes the case that companies who understand their values and who begin with their purpose, inspire their customers, I am making the case that teachers who remain grounded in *their* purpose are most likely to inspire their students. In their introduction to *Kids Deserve It!*, Todd Nesloney and Adam Welcome (2016) write: "Money isn't what draws people to a career in education. People choose education because they want to make a difference—to change lives and impart wisdom to future generations." (xi) It is my hope that the pages of this chapter will remind teachers of their true role in education and will underscore their broader purpose in the classroom. I firmly believe that teachers who remember their "why" have the greatest impact on students, and they are the most fulfilled in their profession.

I did not always want to be a teacher. When I began college in 1988, my major was sociology. I was drawn to social work; specifically, I thought I wanted to be a probation officer. I changed my major to education halfway through my sophomore year after listening to a recording of the 1986 National Teacher of the Year, Guy Doud. In his talk, he shared some of the painful school experiences from his own childhood, as well as the powerful role that a few teachers played in encouraging him and supporting him through school. His poignant talk connected with me on an emotional level as I listened to it over and over. I was moved by his passion and by the power he described in student–teacher relationships. This singular tape recording inspired me to become a teacher. I wanted to make a difference, too!

As a young teacher working in a low-income, urban high school, I remember having a discussion with one of my classes about dreams, ambitions, and life goals. I recall Antonio making a comment that caught me off guard. Referring to his own neighborhood, he exclaimed: "I already know I'm going to live here the rest of my life." He said it with a chuckle, and I remember some of the other students laughing. What I took from his comment was that he felt like the rest of the class was talking about pipe dreams—dreams that were unrealistic and unattainable. That was a profoundly sad moment for me. Years later, I ran into a former student from that same school and, in the course of our conversation, she underscored the same truth that devastated me as a first-year teacher. Some students do not have hope that their situation can be any different than it is right now. Nobody in their family ever went to college, so it is unreasonable for them to think that they could go to college. They do not see education as a "way out" because it has not helped any of their friends or family escape poverty.

If you work in an affluent setting, your dynamics might be a bit different… but that doesn't mean that there is more *hope*. You may have students dealing with depression, eating disorders, substance abuse, or anxiety. There are some students who are suffering from emotional neglect at home. They are not lacking for material possessions, but they do not feel loved. There are students who seem to be well-off by all appearances, but they are not happy. And they cannot envision circumstances changing in their life to make things any better. They do not see a way out either.

As educators, we are not just teaching lessons—we are teaching kids. We want to create brighter futures for our students, but we first need them to envision that brighter future. Teachers have the ability to give students something that is far more valuable than good grades on a report card. They can give them hope. Most kids do not realize how much potential they have. That is where teachers come in. They inspire students with possibilities. They instill in them the belief that they can do more than they ever imagined.

The Sign

As a young assistant principal, I was responsible for discipline. And the disciplinary referrals seemed to be never-ending! It often seemed as though my office was a revolving door, and I was nothing more than a dispenser of consequences. But I wanted more than that. I wanted my interactions with the students to be meaningful. I was reminded of the tradition that a lot of teams had of touching a sign before they leave the locker room. My brother went to the University of Notre Dame, and he had given my sons a replica of the sign that hangs in their football team's locker room. It reads: "PLAY LIKE A CHAMPION TODAY." The messages on these signs are motivational. They are meant to inspire, encourage, and empower.

I thought to myself, "Why couldn't I have a sign like that in my office?" So, I emailed my staff and asked them for feedback: "When students leave my office to come back to your classroom, if they touched a sign before they left my office… what would you want that sign to say?" This is what we came up with:

I AM THE DIFFERENCE!

Our carpentry class made the sign, and I hung it over my door. Over the years, I tried to cultivate a tradition of students touching the sign. To me, this was the ultimate message of empowerment for our students. It is a message that communicates to students that they do not need to be victims of their circumstances. I wanted our students to understand that their behavior and their attitude was the determining factor—whatever the situation might be. I also liked for our teachers to touch the sign. I wanted them to be reminded of the pivotal role that *they* play. *They* are the difference in their classroom. *They* are the difference in our school. *They* are the difference for our students! One year, I gave out bracelets to all our staff members that said: "I am the difference." At one faculty meeting, we even had it written on a cookie cake. This was a theme that I continually emphasized with our faculty. I never wanted our teachers to forget about the potential they had to be difference-makers for their students.

The Wall of Dreams

Several years ago, we mounted a large white board on one of the main hallways of our school. (It was actually two 4' x 8' shower boards that our maintenance technician spliced together.) We called this our "Wall of Dreams," and we asked all of our students to write their dream on the wall. Teachers would walk past this wall on their way to the workroom, and I would remind them periodically to stop and read some of the dreams. As educators, we are focused on student achievement and academic growth. That's a good focus, but I doubt that many of us got into education to raise test scores. We became teachers to make a difference for students. We want to impact the trajectory of their lives. We want to help create brighter futures for them. We want to inspire them and empower our students to chase their dreams. This wall captured the career aspirations of our students, but it also did more than that. It also reflected the tender heart of many of them. These are some of those dreams:

"I want to get better at math."
"My dream is to be a loving mother."
"My dream is for my sister to get out of the Air Force alive."
"I want to do something that MEANS something."
"My dream is to go to Paris, go to UAB, and get my first kiss."
"I want the world to hear my voice."
"I wish my dad would get out of jail."

So, this wall of dreams helped us to keep our focus. It reminded us that our students had passions and struggles that adults in the building knew little about. It served as a daily reminder of why we come to work each day.

Faces Instead of Numbers

I remember popping into some data meetings that our reading and math teachers were having. The reading teachers began with a quick review of spreadsheets. They learned how to manipulate their data (i.e. sorting and filtering) to make it more "teacher friendly." After the refresher on Google Sheets, they looked at how their students had performed on standardized tests last spring. They were able to divide those students into four different groups: exceeding, ready, close, and needs support. Furthermore, they analyzed the results of the recent benchmark assessments to determine how students were currently performing on the essential objectives.

Because the math benchmark has contained the same questions over the last three years, our teachers could actually track the trends on how their students had performed on the same questions. This indepth analysis provided our teachers guidance on how their instruction needed to be tweaked over the coming months. It also revealed which students needed to be targeted with certain objectives. This is the essence of "formative assessment"… and my teachers engaged in it brilliantly.

I was proud of how these teachers used the data to drive their instruction and increase their effectiveness in the classroom… but it was my hope that they never lost sight of this: ultimately, it's not about the data; it's about the kids. I loved seeing my teachers write down the names of students who were one or two points away from proficiency. They recognized that these were not just numbers—they were names; they were faces! It is easy to be bogged down in the numbers, but we must remind ourselves that we are never analyzing "data points;" we are talking about children. Each cell in the spreadsheet represents a student… and all of their potential. Analyzing the data is useful, but we must never lose sight of what that data represents.

Brayden's Story

As I mentioned earlier, one of my favorite things about our school was our wall of dreams. I loved showing this wall to visitors in our building! I wanted them to see the aspirations of the awesome students in our school. And, as I said, I also loved for teachers to walk past this wall and be reminded of their "WHY." This wall was such an uplifting part of our school and definitely a point of pride.

The day that students wrote their dreams on the wall was one of my favorite days of the year. Several years ago, I was headed home on this special day when I received a text from one of my teachers. She sent a picture of one of the dreams with the text, "We might need to address this." You can imagine the mix of emotions I experienced when I saw a picture of this dream:

"To be in Canada far away from this stupid school!"

I will confess that my first emotion was anger. How dare this punk kid write something so negative on our "inspirational" wall. I was also embarrassed that maybe our school's culture wasn't as awesome as I thought it was. But very quickly I was overwhelmed with sadness as I thought about what might have inspired that dream. What would compel an 11-year-old to write that? Maybe he had a teacher embarrass him on the first day of school, and he just couldn't get past it. Maybe other kids were picking on him in the hallway. Maybe he didn't have any friends to sit with him in the lunchroom. I thought of all these scenarios, and none of them were good. None of them were going to be easy to address. But I knew I needed to talk to him.

His name was Brayden. I pulled him into my office, and after a little bit of small talk, I raised the question of his dream; and I asked him why he wanted to leave "this stupid school." I was prepared for him to talk about teachers being mean or other kids bullying him. But that wasn't it at all. He commented to me, somewhat directly, that the hallways were too crowded. He thought there were just too many students. I responded, "Well Brayden, I understand. Our hallways are kind of crowded this year. We do have a lot of students, and I'm sorry, dude, but there's not much I can do about that." So, he never shared anything that I could "fix"… and his feelings about our school did not appear to be as negative as his dream led me to believe. I can't tell you how relieved I was!

But I still needed to find out what his dream was. I said, "Well Brayden… do you mind telling me what your real dream is?" His response floored me.

"I want to be a fifth-grade reading teacher."

I was stunned. I looked at him in disbelief. "Dude! That's the coolest dream I've ever heard!" I literally jumped out of my seat to high-five him. I asked if he would be willing to write the new dream on the wall, and he agreed.

As a principal, I had to know what was behind that dream. When a sixth-grade boy indicates that he wants to become a fifth-grade reading teacher, it cannot be random. I had to figure out who taught him reading the previous year because I felt she would appreciate hearing this story. After all, I cannot think of a more meaningful tribute to a teacher. I was able to track down the teacher. Her name was Katy and, when she taught Brayden the year before, she was a first-year teacher. I shared this story with her and thanked her for the impact she had on Brayden. Her eyes got a little wet as she listened, and when I finished, her response surprised me. She said, "I didn't think he liked school; I didn't think he liked my class or even reading."

So, why is this story important to me, and why do I share it here? I share it because it underscores the potential teachers have to impact the lives of their students. The story of Brayden reminds us that we never know how far our influence will extend. Sometimes, the students might not seem like they're listening. Sometimes, they might not seem like they care. But the teacher's influence is still there. The impact is real. And you might never know how you are making a difference for a student, or how you may be shaping the trajectory of their life.

In his book *Drive*, Daniel Pink (2009) makes the case that research suggests three factors that contribute to human motivation: *Autonomy*—the extent to which one has control and independence over one's work; *Mastery*—the extent to which one feels competent in one's work; and *Purpose*—the extent to which one derives meaning and significance in one's work. Autonomy is, in large part, dependent on school culture and administration; mastery relates to the discussion in Chapter 4 and the commitment to professional growth. *Purpose* has been the theme of this chapter. Pink writes, "The most deeply motivated people—not to mention those who are most productive and satisfied—hitch their desires to a cause larger than themselves." (131) Effective teachers do not forget their cause. They are continually mindful of their purpose and cognizant of their impact on students. They are the ones who are inspired to excel in their work and push through adversity.

It's safe to say that we teachers choose this profession because we want to make a difference, change the world. But then we enter the classroom, and the realization that this job is the epitome of difficult comes crashing down upon us. We then either quit, or we stay in the classroom, dispassionately biding our time until retirement, or we embrace the fact that this job is hard, pull ourselves up by our bootstraps, and decide to change the world anyway.

Notice, students will often complain about the lazy teacher who lets them do nothing. Students may enjoy the nap in these teachers' classes, but they will never re visit them to tell them what a difference they made in their lives. "Rock star" teachers don't let challenges coerce them into complacency. They remember that lives are on the line, what a difference they can make in the life of a child, and simply work longer, love deeper, and fight harder. They recognize their folly in thinking that "changing the world" would require anything other than blood, sweat, and tears but find inspiration in remembering their purpose: to instill love and joy in students who may never have experienced either, even the disrespectful ones who are difficult to love. This is what separates the teachers who bring their "A" game every day from those who are just biding their time until retirement.

Jake Huggins, Teacher

I always knew I wanted to be a teacher. When I was a little girl, I would play school with my brothers and cousins. I was always the teacher and they were the students. My first day of first grade I told my mom that I wanted to be a teacher when I grew up. My passion and desire to teach never wavered and worked in connection with my faith. I wanted to use my gifts and talents to serve the Lord. I knew that was my purpose from a young age.

Whether your story is like mine and you always knew you wanted to be a teacher, whether you decided later in life, or maybe it's a second career, the "Why I chose to be a teacher" stories are remarkable stories and usually include a moment when someone decided that they wanted to make a difference in students' lives. Throughout my career, I have found that you can never lose sight of your purpose. The job of a teacher can seem overwhelming at times with paperwork, state mandates, standardized assessments, collaboration time with colleagues, talking to parents, and of course, teaching, to name a few. Your purpose must be the driving force behind what you do each day. It's what keeps you going, and you cannot lose sight of it. On the days when I feel tired and grouchy, I think to myself, "How do I want my own children to be treated today by their teachers?" And I always answer that question, "I want my children to have a wonderful day with teachers who are caring, understanding, and ready. I want their teacher to be willing to spend time with them if they don't understand and willing to ensure that they are learning—someone excited and happy to be at work that day."

In my experience, I have found that there are two components that connect to my purpose. Creating relationships with students is the foundation of establishing an environment in which they feel safe and comfortable, which connects to student engagement and learning. Students need to know that their teacher cares about them. In addition, teachers must always remember that the ultimate goal for the student is to learn. Because you care for your students, you want them to learn and to be successful. With this goal in mind each day, teachers can make a difference in students' lives, which is usually one of the reasons people decide to become teachers.

Neely Woodley, Educator

6

Knowing Your Students

The iceberg analogy can be a useful one when we think about the students in our classroom. A ship that encounters an iceberg in the north Atlantic sees just the tip of the iceberg. There is typically a massive amount of ice just below the surface. Most of the iceberg is unseen, but it's most definitely there. I wrote an essay in college entitled "There's More to Me Than Meets the Eye." That is an essay every young person could write. What we see in our classrooms is just the "tip of the iceberg." Every student has a story, and it is important that teachers take the time to learn it. As Whitaker (2020) noted, "When a teacher's sensitivity to students increases, so does the opportunity to reach them." That is the theme of this chapter—the importance of teachers understanding their students—knowing their interests, dreams, and challenges.

10 to 15

I'll call him "John." A number of years ago, when I was an assistant principal, John was caught with a bag of weed. That infraction earned him a stay in our alternative school for 45 days. I didn't know John well (he was fairly new to our school), and I knew that my potential to impact him would be negligible when he left our building, so I decided to have a talk with him. Sometimes, when I'm trying to connect with a student, I'll take a walk with them somewhere around campus. On this day, I ended up sitting with John on a concrete picnic table near the stadium. I started in… "John, how many friends do you have outside of school? He responded tersely: "I don't have friends; I have acquaintances." I responded, "Okay, acquaintances. How many guys do you hang with?" He said, "About 10 to 15." I then asked, "Of those 10 to 15 friends, how many would you say smoke weed?" He replied very matter-of-factly, "About 10 to 15."

Two realizations hit me like a ton of bricks. First, this kid doesn't stand a chance if he doesn't find a new group of friends. And second, it is almost impossible for adults alone to counter-act the influence of peer groups. John could have the most com-passionate teachers in the world. They may be outstanding role models who care about him and strive to motivate him to make good decisions in life. But when the 3:00 pm bell rings, the posi-tive messages he hears in the school are quickly drowned out by the influences on the streets of his neighborhood. We want kids to reject temptations like illicit drugs because there is a whole other world out there for them. But what if—as far as they know—there isn't? What if their entire world is defined by the ubiquity of weed and everything that goes with it? As educators, we need to remain mindful of what our students are exposed to outside of our classroom. They often feel pressure from all sides—peer groups, social media, and, sometimes, simply in their own home. It is important that teachers consider how these influences shape who their students are and how they respond in the classroom.

The Girl with Red Hair

She was just being defiant. I was certain I needed to suspend her. She had streaks of bright red hair—like fire engine red! We had a large high school of 1800 students, but I was in the hallway a lot, and I couldn't help but notice the hair. I casually warned her a few times that she would need to change the color of her hair because our code of conduct didn't allow "unnatural hair color." Several days passed, and I still noticed the hair. As an experienced administrator, I knew I had bigger battles to fight, so I always tried to steer clear of "going to the mat" over dress code violations but, at this point, it seemed like she was being defiant. So, I confronted her during a class change. I told her I didn't want to suspend her, but she seemed to be flaunting our student code of conduct, and I thought she was leaving me no choice. I basically said to her, "What's your deal!?" Her eyes got wet, and I could tell she felt shame just having to talk to me. (She was never in trouble, had never been sent to the office, and, aside from the hair color, went totally under the radar.) She went on to share the personal drama she was having to live through at home. She finally said something that knocked the wind out of me: "Dr. Steele, I feel like the color of my hair is the only thing in my life that I can control."

This is a moment that I will not forget. As I write these words, my eyes are welling up… thinking about this young lady's feelings of desperation… thinking about the lives that many of our students are living… thinking about the challenges confronting many of the kids in our schools—challenges completely unknown to the adults in the building. When I heard her story, my preoccupation with hair color suddenly seemed absurd. I know we need rules. And students have to be held accountable for following the rules. I get it. But it is vital that we take the time to hear and actually *feel* the story of our students. We will never understand our students if we don't stop to genuinely listen. But we can't just listen to their story; we have to actually care about their story. When we do that, our perspective will forever be altered. That is when we can connect with students; that is when we can impact students; that is when we have the chance to really make a difference.

Worlds Collide

A number of years ago, when I was an assistant principal, I vividly remember spending about an hour talking with one of our 18-year-old students. He grew up in a poor neighborhood but, through a variety of circumstances, had been attending an affluent, mostly white, suburban high school for the last few years. He had been in a lot of trouble at school, but he was scheduled to graduate that year. That week, his teacher had been particularly aggravated with him because he didn't show up for the ACT that she had helped him register for. He ended up in my office on this day because he and his teacher "got into it." When I asked him about not showing up for the ACT, he finally admitted that he didn't want to go to college. Eventually, he admitted that he was scared to go to college. (Keep in mind that no one in his family had ever gone to college, or maybe even graduated from high school.) I explained that his education and the help of his teachers were allowing for him to have a different life. He responded that he didn't *want* a different life. In so many words, he indicated that he would never feel comfortable in *my* middle class world. He said, *"Dr. Steele, I'll tell you the truth… If I became the richest man in the world right now, I'd build a big house right in the middle of the hood… because that's where I'm comfortable."*

I was reminded that none of his teachers could imagine what it was like to be in his shoes… and he was scared to death to walk a mile in my "middle class" shoes. I told him that anything is possible, and that my hope was that he would choose a path that he really wanted, and that his decisions would not be based on fear. We hugged, and we both cried. That probably wasn't professional. But I didn't care.

Mountains to Climb

Early in my career as an administrator, I remember being frustrated with a 16-year-old boy named Cedric. He was defiant, belligerent, and seemed to have no respect for authority. He always had a chip on his shoulder and had no trouble maintaining his tough image with me. He was what we called "hard." I prided myself on building relationships with students, but I could never get him to let down his guard. I had run out of patience with him, and I confess that I had sort of written him off. One day in my office, I decided to give it another go. I said, "Cedric, we all have challenges in life; we all have mountains that we have to climb. What challenges do you have in your life?" I was not prepared for what he told me. Cedric's demeanor became a little softer as he said, "I don't have anyone to take care of me." This is a moment I will never forget.

Cedric lived with his 80-year-old invalid grandmother, and she was not able to do much. She certainly was unable to provide the kind of support, guidance, and supervision that 16-year-olds need. I had been upset with this kid for skipping class to play basketball and then being disrespectful when he was caught. As I sat in my office listening to him describe his home situation, I thought to myself, "How is this guy even showing up to school?"

I have often wondered how he is doing. I only worked in that school for one year, so I have not seen him since then. I know that guy had the deck stacked against him, though. I wish all of his teachers knew his story. I hope he had some teachers who were more understanding than me. Every student has a "story," and some of those stories will break your heart. Many students have a hard home life and, sometimes, that shows up as a bad attitude at school. We can't forget there is always something going on behind that "bad attitude." When I think of students like Cedric, I'm reminded of why we do what we do. I'm reminded that we see students every day who desperately need our time, our support, and, indeed, our love. Students walk our halls; they sit in our classes; and we have no idea what they're dealing with. We get frustrated when they're tardy, when they're out of dress code, when they are not prepared, when they are inattentive and disengaged. We must remember that some students have tall mountains to climb. We cannot climb the mountains for them, but an awareness of the mountain reminds us of the importance of our patience and support.

Who Do You Trust?

Early one morning, a "twitter challenge" caught my eye. It was from Leigh Ragsdale (@leighmragsdale), a principal in Missouri. This challenge struck a chord with me. It seemed like a valuable activity. When you are aware of a good idea, I've learned that it's good to go ahead and implement it if you are able. Don't wait! Don't procrastinate! So, after I finished the morning announcements that day, I asked all our students to get out a sheet of paper, and write down the name of one adult that they trusted—someone that they could talk to if they needed. I told them that if they could not think of one, they could write "nobody." I collected all the papers, and we began putting our data into a spreadsheet.

Out of about 500 students, we had 38 who wrote "nobody." That's 38 too many! We wanted every student to feel connected in our school, as I know you do in your school. We wanted every child to have an adult they feel comfortable talking to.

I made a slide show of the pictures of our students that wrote "nobody", and we watched it at our next faculty meeting. There were no names attached to any of the pictures, and we did not discuss who taught these students. (Our students all had seven or eight different teachers, so everyone taught some of these students.) We viewed these pictures in complete silence. It was a sobering moment—one that I will not soon forget. When it was over, I told our teachers, "It is my hope that if we do this activity in a few months, we won't have any students who write "nobody." Some of the students were predictable. They were loners, or they were constantly in trouble. But there were other students that evoked audible gasps from our staff when their pictures appeared on the screen. These students made good grades; they were "good kids." Surely they had good relationships with their teachers. Here's the thing: it's not enough for teachers to think they have a personal connection with a student; students have to *feel* that connection. And we can never take those relationships for granted.

Memories from Third Grade

I have two vivid memories from third grade. The first one is that I was the fastest kid in the class. At field day that year, each of the eight third-grade classes sent a representative to the 50 yard dash. I won! To a third-grade boy, this was a big deal. Bruce

Springsteen sings a song about "Glory Days." Well mine were in the third grade… and they certainly passed me by. But I had another memory. My reading teacher that year always seemed to give me grief about not having my homework. I had two loving parents; they read to me, encouraged me, and generally helped me stay on top of my school work. But that year was a stressful one at the Steele household. We went through a tornado; our car was totaled; our home was broken into; we were flooded out of our house; and my dad was unemployed part of the year. That year, my mom didn't have the wherewithal to ensure I always had my homework completed. And I always heard about it during reading class. I don't know that my teacher was trying to embarrass me, but that was always the effect. I still remember the shame. Teachers need to remember that they're not just teaching lessons; they're creating memories for their students, and some of those memories will last a lifetime.

More Than Meets the Eye

Every school in America has challenging students, and virtually every teacher in our schools is confronted with these students at some point during the day. Some of them are challenging because they never come to class prepared. Some are challenging because they can't sit still. Some are challenging because they always seem to have a chip on their shoulder. Some are challenging because of their disrespectful attitude. And then some students are challenging because they just do not seem to care about anything.

But consider this: while there are teachers at every school who complain about these students at the lunch table or in the teacher's lounge, those schools have teachers who experience success with those same students. Those students are a thorn in the side of the first group of teachers, yet they are a source of professional satisfaction with the second group. So, what is the difference?

Some teachers realize the student who never comes to class prepared might not have a lot of support at home. Maybe the student is disorganized and irresponsible, but when the student shows up without a pencil, they give her a pencil. They don't make a thing of it because they realize there are better ways to teach responsibility. And they certainly do not want anything to be a barrier to class participation.

Some teachers realize that the student who cannot sit still does not like getting in trouble; he just has an overabundance of energy. (I know adults who can't sit still for 45 minutes, and I bet you do, too.) I remember one of our teachers who made a deal with one of these energetic students that he could stand up and do his work as long as he got it done. The deal worked like magic.

Some teachers realize that the student with a chip on her shoulder has had a miserable school experience. She hasn't found anything she feels good about in school, so she doesn't have healthy ways of getting attention. Those teachers go out of their way to show respect to these students and affirm them as often as possible. They do not engage in petty "battles" in the classroom because they understand that, when there is a battle in the classroom, nobody wins.

Some teachers realize that the student's disrespectful attitude likely has nothing to do with the teacher. They do not lower their standards, but they also do not take everything personally. These teachers work to build positive rapport on the first day of school, so antagonistic attitudes never even take root.

Some teachers realize that the students who do not seem to care about anything may not be as apathetic as they seem. These teachers have a conviction that no student wants to fail, no student likes being in trouble, and no student wants to be labeled a "loser." They recognize that each student cares about something, but maybe the adults in the building just have not figured out what it is, or how to cultivate it. Maybe these students just do not see the relevance of school, so these teachers work harder to make their class meaningful. Maybe these students are tired of not being good enough at school; they find that not trying is preferable to encountering failure yet again. It can be a shield to protect themselves from embarrassment. So, these teachers are relentless about supporting the students and finding little ways for them to experience success. They know that the little successes can eventually turn into big successes. In *Be the One for*

Kids, Ryan Sheehy (2018) writes, "When educators invest the time to learn their students' stories, they have a better understanding of what motivates them. With that knowledge, it becomes easier to empower them to succeed."

> Understanding students as individuals is not a direct link to higher test scores. It is far more important: it is a direct link to expanded humanity. The sulky fringe-dweller, the showy intellectual, the cranky prankster, and all such camouflages can be quite exploded with free-writes and follow-ups. Offering prompts that invite students to share fears, joys, failings, and hopes leads to understanding the human beneath the facade. Over the decades, I have learned about—and responded to—addiction, abuse, food insecurity, and illness. Teacher involvement must be careful, respectful, and aligned with policies and laws, of course, but these guarded interventions developed into life-changing relationships. Reflective prompts aren't simply fishing for trouble. Discovery of poets, artists, philanthropists, athletes, et al., got me out of the classroom to see fair-to-middlin' English students totally rock in activities that bring them true joy. That shared delight is life-changing, too. Across disciplines, giving students the chance to respond confidentially to prompts as simple as "What obstacles did you face while doing your [geometry/physics] work last night?" may open the door to understanding the whole person occupying your classroom for a year… or if you're lucky, the person who's in your life for years to come.
>
> Renee Brown, Teacher

I began teaching with the mindset of, "I'm the teacher, and students will do as I say because I have the 'authority.'" Consequently, I was constantly frustrated that some students didn't recognize the authority bestowed upon me by my B.S. degree. "Aaron" was one such student. Extremely hyperactive, Aaron acted as though he had never been outside, and he fought constantly for my class's attention. It wasn't until his father showed up to open house, drunk and cursing at both Aaron and me, that I realized that my authority wasn't high on Aaron's priorities list. After Aaron had just seen his father arrested for disorderly conduct, I hugged him, saying, "I'm sorry that you have to deal with this." He replied joyfully, as though nothing had happened, "It's no problem Mr. Turner, I'm used to it. I burst out crying, losing my need for "authority" and finding compassion. Instead of being irritated by Aaron's energy, I refocused it by having him read aloud, run errands, or whatever else I could do to give him the positive attention he so desperately needed. Students need more than academic knowledge; they need an advocate who is willing to take the time to understand them. It is at this point that they are open to learning.

Joe Turner, Teacher

7

Building Relationships

Just because it said so on the syllabus, or because the teacher rou-
tinely proclaims to the entire class: "You guys know how much I
love you", doesn't mean students understand that their teachers
care about them. Students know their teachers care about them
by how they treat them: they cannot just say it; they have to show
it. When you talk to your students outside of your classroom,
you show it. When your students are having a bad day and you
demonstrate compassion, you show it. When they lose a loved
one and you call and check on them, or maybe even visit them,
you show it.

Just as effective teachers are relentless about finding resources
and strategies to ensure students learn the material, they are also
determined to find ways to demonstrate care and make personal connections with them in order to build the relationship.
And these teacher–student relationships are not valuable simply
because they make students feel good while they're in school and
teachers feel gratified about connecting with kids. The research
of John Hattie (2009) demonstrates that these relationships have
a high impact on student learning.

A successful high school coach in our area used to tell
younger coaches: "Don't worry about winning games; win the
kids. If you win the kids, the games will take care of themselves."
Consider how this applies to your classroom. Of course, I realize

that the lessons will never actually "take care of themselves," but this quote underscores the importance of "winning over the students." The teachers that understand this reality, the ones who do the work to forge meaningful relationships with their students, these are the ones who have the biggest impact in the classroom. And these are the teachers who will be remembered. There is no formula for building relationships with students; effective teachers work at it and make it a priority. It is my hope that the stories and strategies in this chapter will energize your efforts.

Standing at the Door

Technology has replaced a lot of things in the classroom. It will never replace a smiling teacher, greeting kids as they walk into class. When teachers connect with their students as they enter the room, they provide a "hook" that will probably be more meaningful than the bell-ringer. Every time we give a student a high-five, a fist bump, a handshake, or a hug, we are telling them, "You matter." School is stressful, and sometimes it's hard being a kid. Students have drama at home, drama on the school bus, and drama in the hallway. When they are able to make a personal connection with the teacher as they walk into class, it can go a long way toward injecting positivity into their day. A genuine greeting at the door can set the tone for the class, can put the student in a positive frame of mind, and can even change the trajectory of a student's bad day.

Lifelines

When a former colleague of mine, Joe Turner, was named "Teacher of the Year," a reporter asked him for his advice to new teachers. He responded: *"Teach every child like you're their lifeline… like you're their last chance to succeed."* When I read this, it shook me to my core. I shared it with our leadership team and it inspired an initiative at our school that we simply called "Lifelines." This was not a formal program; it was not structured, and there was no paperwork. We simply asked our staff members to be a lifeline to one or two students who would benefit from an adult in their corner. As a faculty, we committed to going above and beyond to care about these students.

As a principal, I also had several lifelines. One of my challenges with this project was that I did not teach these students. I did not necessarily even see them every day. The hallways were crowded, so class changes were not always great opportunities to have conversations with students. And it can sometimes be awkward calling kids into the office just to check on them.

But I had an idea—a new strategy for making regular connections with my three students. It was outside of the box, but I needed to try something different. I called Caleb down to the office and said, "Caleb... will you do me a favor?" He smiled and nodded, "Yes." I continued, "I usually have good days, but not always. Everyone can benefit from a friend checking on them. Will you do me a favor and check on me every day, just to make sure I'm doing alright." He smiled again and said "Okay."

I had this conversation with my two other students as well, and the results absolutely fired me up. These three students started making regular eye contact with me in the halls, they were smiling at me, and they were asking me about my day. This gave me a regular opportunity to connect with them, and it taught them to think about the well-being of someone other than themselves.

Lefty

There was a student named Cortez who was always in trouble and was always in the office. (His real name was Lefty, but he went by Cortez.) In particular, he was constantly being written up by Ms. Johnson. I assigned Cortez detention, I assigned him in-school suspension, and I suspended him. As often as he was in my office, he received a lot of discipline from me. But he and I had a great relationship. For years, my classroom and then my office was decorated with a picture of Michael Jordan. Cortez loved basketball, and virtually every time he was in my office, he asked if he could have that poster of Jordan. His dream was to make the JV basketball team. He was not quite five feet tall in the ninth grade and, from what I heard, did not have a lot of ability. But basketball was his passion. So, we would talk about basketball.

By about February of that year, Ms. Johnson came to see me, and she was exasperated. She vented, "I just don't know what to do with Cortez! Do you have any suggestions?" I responded, "Ms. Johnson, do you know what Cortez's dream is?" She didn't. I went on, "Ms. Johnson, his dream is to make the JV basketball team." So, I suggested to her that she take some time to get to know Cortez—to connect with him on a personal level.

The teachers who have the biggest impact on kids practice empathy. They do not just teach their students; they try to understand them. I know a lot of teachers have students fill out personal information on index cards on the first day of school. That is a great practice, but we have to use the information the students tell us. It gives us a window into their world. It can provide the groundwork for developing a relationship. If you want students to take an interest in your class, start by taking an interest in them. When students feel a connection to their teacher, they are much more likely to care about the lesson. And when they have a good relationship with their teacher, they are always less likely to misbehave in class. If Ms. Johnson understood and appreciated Cortez's love for basketball back in September, I suspect her entire year could have gone differently.

Noticing the Little Things

How often have you heard another teacher complain about a student, saying something like, "She's just doing that for attention," or "He's just trying to get the other kids to look at him."? Well… it is normal to want attention. We all want to be noticed; we all want to matter. When students are getting some attention for the right reasons, they are less likely to seek attention in inappropriate ways. Some kids have good smiles; some ask good questions; some are good at magic; some are creative; some are good helpers; some can remember lines from TV shows; some can make kids laugh; some have great handwriting. Every kid can do something well! Figure out what it is. It is important to catch kids being good and recognize them. Students need attention, and they will get it, one way or another. So, one way to cultivate relationships with students is to be relentless about noticing and acknowledging them… even for little things.

I remember hearing a famous comedian describe his experience in middle school. He was continually in trouble for being the "class clown." One day, his teacher told him that if he would work hard every day, she would allow him to entertain the class for the last five minutes of class. As the comedian recalled it, the arrangement worked brilliantly. She got work out of him, and it obviously made an impact on the trajectory of this young man's life.

Connecting with a Hobby

When I was a 22-year-old aspiring teacher, I was hired to tutor a student in an alternative school for the last few months of the school year. I was supposed to teach a 15-year-old whose behavior and attitude were so severe that he was not able to make it in his regular school. I think it was fair to say that he had been quite challenging to his previous teachers. I do not recall much about our first meeting, but I do remember he came in with what seemed like quite a chip on his shoulder. I think he wore a black T-shirt with the image of a heavy metal band; he had on black combat boots and his hair was halfway down his back. I quickly figured out that I needed to develop some rapport with this young man, or our relationship would never be productive or positive. If I did not make a connection with him, we might both be in for a long couple of months. I found out that he loved music, he loved playing the guitar, and his favorite musician was Alice Cooper. I asked him if he would bring his guitar to school and teach me some chords. I found an old guitar that I could bring and, in between our school work, he started teaching me to play. Sometimes, I would practice while he would work. I even learned part of an Alice Cooper song.

The weeks rolled by uneventfully, and he successfully finished his time in the alternative school. There is no doubt in my mind that the time together would not have been nearly as productive if we had not talked about music—if we had not played a little bit of guitar together. More than 25 years later and I still know those guitar chords that he taught me. I think about that experience in the alternative school from time to time, and I am reminded about the importance of meeting students where they are, without judgment or condescension.

Showing Up

I remember the evening well. As soon as my daughter got into the car after the volleyball game, she exclaimed, "Dad, my teacher came to my game!" Oftentimes, what students find meaningful about school is the personal connections they have with certain teachers. They always remember the ones that took the time to show an interest in them—to really get to know them. This includes getting to know what they are involved in outside of school. Frankly, what the students are involved in outside of school may be the most important thing to them. It is probably what they are most passionate about. So, when you take the time to show up to a concert, or a play, or a game, it demonstrates that you're trying to enter "their world." The students will notice you, and it will make an impression on them. And, more than likely, it will make an impression on their parents as well.

I know that teachers have personal lives, and chances are they may have their own child's events to attend. But when they can find the time to support their students at those extracurricular events, it goes a long way toward developing rapport with the students and generating goodwill with the parents. When teachers support their students outside the classroom, those students will be more likely to support that teacher inside the classroom.

Meeting the Challenge

There is an element of the "self-fulfilling prophecy" that plays out in teacher–student relationships. Our attitude toward students will affect the way we interact with them in subtle and not so subtle ways. When we are aggravated with a student, we are a little more irritable with her, a little less patient, and a little less gracious. On the flip side, we are extraordinarily patient and flexible with our favorite students; we always give them the benefit of the doubt. When teachers begin extending those same courtesies to the challenging students, they often notice that those students respond positively. Students rise and fall to our expectations. The student that seemingly always gets on our last nerve actually has a lot of potential. That is what we must remind ourselves. That is what we must focus on. When we look for good qualities, we can surprise ourselves with how many we find. If you start treating your most challenging students as though they are your favorite students, over time, they might start acting like your favorites.

Some students carry around with them the burden of a bad reputation. When teachers are looking at rosters before the school year starts, some names may look familiar. They may complain to a colleague, "Oh, I taught his older brother, and he's probably just as bad." Or, "I've heard about her; and I've heard her parents are crazy too!" It is easy for educators to allow reputations and hearsay to shape our opinions and our expectations of the year to come. To be sure, some students have a history of making poor choices, and it would appear that they have earned their "reputation."

Effective teachers allow *their* new year to be a new year for their students as well. They ignore the gossip and refuse to accept the traditional narrative for these kids. The high expectations of these teachers allow these students the opportunity to build a new reputation—to write for themselves a new story. Every student deserves that chance. We all make mistakes, but all of us deserve a fresh start—a shot at redemption. YOU can be that teacher who helps the students "turn the corner." Ultimately, reaching students that are "hard-to-reach" is not about having the right strategy… it's about having the right heart. It's a relentless passion for connecting with kids.

Starting with Care

There are 101 ways to connect with your students. But none of them work if you don't begin with care. And, if you have that, you can make almost any strategy work. It is easy to talk about the priority of building relationships with students. Most of us would agree that it is important, but some may not have a good handle on how to go about making it happen. The good news is, anyone can make it happen! It starts with a genuine desire to connect with your students. You then spend time talking to them. And I do not mean talking to them about the material you are teaching. Ask them about their family, their friends, their interests outside of school, and maybe even the stuff that aggravates them. What do they care about? PokemonGo, Fortnite, slime, TickTok, fidget spinners? I recommend that teachers engage with students about things that *they* care about.

These interactions with students do not necessarily have to be about personal interests, however. As Schlechty (2011) notes, the lesson and the learning can serve as the foundation:

How do teachers communicate to students that they believe in them and trust them?
There is no magic formula here. I have observed, however, that teachers who find the time to engage students in personal conversations and conduct interviews with students to reveal that the teacher wants to ensure that work students are expected to do is engaging increases trust between students and the teacher. (25)

You will probably not bond with your students after just one personal conversation. It usually does not work that way. Relationships take time. But if you persist with authentic and personal interactions, you will form a connection. Most students appreciate it when their teachers take an interest in them. When they feel as though you like them—as though you really do care about them, they will usually reciprocate with some positive interactions of their own. But it always starts with the teacher and a genuine care for the students.

Teachers can prepare their students for the test without building meaningful relationships with them—but the test result is not the only goal of a good teacher. When graduates come back to visit teachers, they visit the ones who took an interest in them. You see, the legacy of great teachers is not usually found in the lessons they taught their students… rather, it is in the relationships they built with their students. Lesson plans are important and pedagogy matters, but some of the most important work of teachers might not be captured by a plan. When teachers encourage, support, inspire, care about, and connect with their students, they are engaged in work that transcends the "plan." Every time you interact with a student, you have the opportunity to make them feel special. Remember that all those interactions you have with your students outside of the lesson really matter. And, in some cases, the personal connections are what makes the learning even possible.

> Building relationships with the students that I teach is EVERYTHING to me and a must in this profession. Building relationships is crucial for me because once the kids know that you truly love and care about them as a person, they will want to do better. By them knowing you care about them as a person first and not just another student, leads to them not wanting to let you down, better behavior, and wanting to succeed for you. Getting to know the students personally allows you to understand them so much better and why they might do or not do certain things at school. Once you get to know their stories as a teacher it allows you to see the students in a different light. I always try to find ONE thing that I have in common with every student and then that is my in. I never force a student to talk to me when I get the vibe they don't feel like sharing, but I will continue to try every couple of days until the student finally does. Once I find that one common thing I just go from there and so do the students. We might stay on that one topic for a week or longer, but it usually always ends up to the students sharing more and more about themselves because they know that I care. I have built relationships with students by talking about sports, my parents being divorced just like theirs, video games, movies, etc.
>
> This year I made a connection with a student that would never speak in class or to other students. I would

make sure I would always say "Hi" to him and ask how he was doing and I would get the same answer every day. He would just look down to the ground and say "Hi" back and say "Good" every day. Whenever we went outside for PE the students would have an option to walk with their friends. He chose to walk by himself every day that we went outside. One day I decided to walk with him and he looked at me like I was crazy. I just walked and asked how he was doing and how school was going and he quietly answered me. I then asked the question about what does he enjoy to do outside of school? Movies? Video games? Sports? Pets? Netflix? He said I love playing survival horror video games and watching scary movies! Little did he know that I used to love survival horror games and horror movies also!! We started to talk about the video games and then finally got to Friday the 13th movies and that's when it all changed. EVERY single day he comes up to me now during class to ask me how I am doing, if I have watched any new horror movies lately, and many other questions. We now have a relationship and I can tell he likes the class so much more just by knowing that we have a connection and I know him as a person. Bottom line is, if I never walked with him that day, I would have never known what he likes and doesn't like, and we wouldn't have a relationship at all. Some students might have numerous relationships throughout the day and some may have none. Some students' home lives are not good at all, so I try to make a connection with every single student and let them know that I care about them. I might be the only adult relationship they have in their lives and them knowing that I care about them is what matters most to me.

Grant Urbanski, Teacher

'You have to be really mean until Christmas.' That was the advice I received over and over before starting my first year of teaching. I tried it and I was miserable. Over my 11 years of teaching I have learned how terrible that advice really was for building relationships. I read a book two summers ago about a girl who had a horrible home life, no reliable food, no help with homework, no parental support and so many of her basic needs not met. After reading that, I decided that none of my "kids" would ever be in that position on my watch and I would make sure they knew that. I now start day one every semester telling students about my classroom expectations, but then telling them about the section of my room that I have with toiletries, snacks, water and a comment box for any additional needs. I tell them how much I absolutely love them and that the reason I teach is because I believe in them. I'm very clear on my expectations for respect within my walls. Some of the toughest kids just really want to be loved and cared for. They need structure and discipline—so don't cave on those things for the sake of being "nice." But make sure that they understand that even if they mess up, they are loved. Support their interests, attend their games, help them when they struggle and praise them when they don't give up.

Katie Mantel, Teacher

During my years in education I have had the opportunity to work with students from multiple cultures and socio economic statuses. When it comes to building relationships with students, they all want the same things: to feel loved, to have a safety net, discipline and direction. Yes, DISCIPLINE! People like and need discipline, rules and boundaries. They bring stability to society. The key as educators is to know how and when to use it. You cannot expect to be a drill sergeant from day one without knowing your students first. If we do not know what triggers them and what motivates them, we WILL NOT get the response we want. MOST educators may read this and think, "How I am going to have time to get to know ALL of my students?"

You must MAKE TIME! If you want to be the best at your calling, GET TO KNOW YOUR STUDENTS! You can do this with a simple first day "get to know each other" activity. Ask students to write or verbalize questions like, "What city are you from?" "Have you attended our schools your entire life?" "If not, what school do you come from?" "Who do you live with?" "Do you have any siblings?" Basic questions like these will provide personal information and spark a caring relationship. IT WILL BE WORTH YOUR TIME. LOVE your students, GET TO KNOW THEM!

Frankie Perez, Teacher

Part III
The Third Dimension
The School Cultural Perspective

8

Transforming Your School

"When the principal sneezes, the whole school catches a cold." As a school leader, this line from Todd Whitaker (2020: 25) always resonated with me. Without a doubt, school culture starts at the top. But while the principal sets the tone for the entire building, no principal creates school culture in a vacuum. School culture is a function of the values, attitudes, and behaviors of ALL the adults in the building. And classrooms are where the magic happens. They are where school culture is built or destroyed. While the most important role for teachers is to *teach* the students in their classroom, they should never underestimate their potential for impacting the culture of the school. Teachers are never neutral with respect to a school's culture. Everyday, the words, actions, and attitudes of teachers either undermine or enhance the mission of the school.

Several years ago, I was visiting another school. It had a great feel, and I saw some very effective teachers. I remember asking one of the teachers about her experiences at the school. I will never forget her response: "When you're surrounded by superstars, it makes you want to be better than you are." Her comment speaks to the power of positive peer pressure within a faculty, and it certainly underscores the potential every teacher has to inspire his or her colleagues.

Many educators are familiar with "The Starfish Story," adapted from an essay by Loren Eisely (1978).

> One day a man was walking along the beach when he noticed a boy picking something up and gently throwing it into the ocean. Approaching the boy, he asked, "What are you doing?" The youth replied, "Throwing starfish back into the ocean. The surf is up and the tide is going out. If I don't throw them back, they'll die." "Son," the man said, "Don't you realize there are miles and miles of beach and hundreds of starfish? You can't make a difference!" After listening politely, the boy bent down, picked up another starfish, and threw it back into the surf. Then, smiling at the man, he said… "I made a difference for that one."

I remember the day our math teachers came into my office to give me a starfish they had made out of construction paper and decorated with glitter. They were excited about their idea and wanted to share it with me. It involved shuffling around their lunch classes and sacrificing some of their "down time" to allow for strategic tutoring of some of their students who were struggling academically. They brought rosters with names highlighted, and they talked through the logistics of how it could work. As I held that paper starfish, I could not have been more proud to be their principal. It meant they understood that our work was about more than just raising academic achievement. They knew this initiative would help kids. Just like the boy throwing a single starfish back into the sea, my math teachers were committed to making a difference for their students… one kid at a time.

In Chapter 5, we talked about the importance of teachers remaining mindful of their core purpose—making a difference for their students. In this final chapter, I highlight some ways that teachers can inspire their colleagues and make a difference in the culture of their school.

Model the Mission

How do you respond to your most challenging students? Most teachers have some difficult students at some point during the day, and it can be tempting to complain about them in the lounge, at the lunch table, in the hallways, or even at faculty meetings. The students are too loud; they won't stop horseplaying; they won't follow directions; they are too disrespectful; they never do their homework; they never come to class prepared; they won't study; they're spoiled by their parents. When you give in to the temptation to complain about these students, there is an impact that is felt beyond your own personal motivation. Your negativity can undermine the focus and sense of purpose of the teachers who are around to hear you vent.

But, on the other hand, when you demonstrate empathy toward your challenging students—when you understand that the inappropriate behaviors are a manifestation of dysfunctional circumstances outside of school, you help to set a different tone in your building. And your attitude toward the students will likely not go unnoticed by other teachers. It is usually the case that the most difficult kids need the most TLC. Your patience with these students reminds other teachers what is really important; it reminds them of *their* purpose—making a difference in the lives of kids.

Bring the Energy

Your child was up all night with an ear infection; you spilled your coffee on the way to school; the copy machine ran out of toner when you were scrambling to finish your copies for the day. There are a million things that could ruin your day, sapping all your energy and all your joy. Remember the picture in my office of Michael Jordan. It is a picture of him jumping from the free throw line to dunk a basketball. I added a caption to the picture, that reads: "What are YOU rising above?" We cannot always control our circumstances, but we can always control our response to those circumstances. Are you a victim of your circumstances or do you choose to rise above them? Your attitude does not just affect your own emotional well-being, it affects everyone around you. It is felt at the lunch table, in the hallway, in the workroom, in the faculty meeting, not to mention in your classroom. Perhaps the best thing teachers can do for their colleagues is to bring a positive attitude to work every day.

It is possible to stay upbeat… even in the face of adversity. We all have tough days, and some circumstances seem to conspire against us. But we can still smile, we can remain optimistic, and we can figure out a way to remind our colleagues "the glass is half full." Optimism is contagious. So is pessimism. Which one do we want to permeate the school? The positive energy you bring to work each day will lift the spirits of those around you. Your commitment to maintaining a positive outlook will generate positive energy in the building that can make the naysayers irrelevant.

Several years ago I was going through a rough patch; I was discouraged. My brother was aware of my struggles and mailed me a hand written note. It began: "Dear Brother—We never know what a year will bring. But we know what *we* will bring. We will bring the Awesome! That will leave the year to fend for itself." That note is now framed, and it sits in my office. You can imagine how it lifted my spirits. Just think about how you can lift the spirits of your colleagues if you bring that type of attitude and energy to work every day.

Own Your Results

Take responsibility for your students' academic achievement, and share your data with colleagues. Data is used by the most successful schools to make instructional decisions and drive school improvement efforts. It is not always comfortable to share your assessment results, but it is an essential component of healthy professional learning communities. When you take the potentially scary steps of sharing your data with colleagues, it encourages others to follow suit. Your candor sends the message that weaknesses will be confronted head on. Faculties that are honest with each other about student achievement are in the best position to do something about it. Do not wait on the principal or instructional coach to call a data meeting—you can start the conversation. It will make it more likely that your colleagues will share their own data as well.

Take Risks

Be willing to take risks… and fail publicly. It is easy for faculties to become complacent, especially when the status quo is adequate. Try something new in your classroom, and let your colleagues know how it goes. If a new activity or strategy does not work out as you had hoped, scrap it… or tweak it, but share your experiences and move on. Your courage and your transparency will inspire other teachers to break out of their own ruts. Innovation thrives in schools where teachers have the courage to fail.

Befriend Your Colleagues

How are their own kids doing? What are their hobbies outside of school? What was their favorite family vacation? What are their plans for the weekend? What book are they reading? Why did they get into education? I know that teachers have a life outside of school and this includes their own set of friends. I realize that the teacher down the hall does not have to be your "BFF." But when your colleagues *become* your friends, work can be a lot more enjoyable. When you get to know your colleagues not just as educators, but as people, it becomes much more likely that your professional relationship will become not just cordial, but close. As you get to know your fellow teachers, your empathy for them will increase, and your collegiality will be strengthened. Your professional relationship will not just be collaborative, but mutually supportive. These relationships do not happen accidentally, however. They grow when educators make a conscious choice to connect with their peers on a personal level. And the camaraderie that can develop among teachers can go a long way toward increasing their level of enjoyment at work and their own sense of professional satisfaction.

Give the Benefit of the Doubt

A lot happens in the school day, and teachers are pulled in a million directions. They are constantly bombarded with announcements, emails, and student questions. Perhaps none of us are as careful with our words as we need to be. We are not always careful to communicate how or what we intend. Maybe the teacher seemed terse with you at the department meeting. Perhaps when you read your colleague's email, it seemed to have a tone that didn't sit right with you. In this context, I think it's helpful when teachers extend grace to one another—to be patient with one another. In the course of a chaotic day, with the myriad of interactions that consume every educator, there is always the potential for misunderstandings. There is always the chance that someone's feelings will be hurt. These challenges can be mitigated when teachers give their colleagues the benefit of the doubt. Recognize that your colleague is busy. Understand that they may be in the middle of a stressful situation. Remember that they love their students just as you do. Believe that they want to excel in their job, just as you do. In the same way that school leaders should assume the best intentions of their teachers, teachers should do the same for their colleagues. When teachers embrace this attitude they help to create a work environment that is healthier for everyone.

Be that Teammate

Teachers love it when their administration has their back. They love it when their fellow teachers have their back as well. When your colleague wakes up sick, but you get their lesson plan together and make copies for the sub, you are their hero. When you cover another teacher's class during your planning period so they can attend their child's performance, you make their day. When you help a teacher work through some challenging classroom management challenges, you make their day a little easier. When you sit with a colleague during a dicey parent conference, you are providing invaluable moral support. Teaching can be an overwhelming profession at times, but supportive and loyal colleagues can be a game changer. Be the teammate you would like to have on *your* team!

Focus on Solutions

Every school has problems. Every teacher will probably have many opportunities each day to get aggravated. Imagine the following two scenarios. In the first one, the teacher approaches the principal and says:

> I don't know why we even bother to have school rules because nobody follows them! Everywhere I turn, a student is walking down the hall on their phone! They're not even supposed to have their phones out but it's like they don't even care!

In the second one, the teacher approaches the principal and says:

> I've noticed a lot of students walking down the halls on their phones lately. At our next leadership team meeting, could we revisit this issue? We might need to tweak our process for handling this behavior and clarify the process for communicating our expectations to students.

Do you see a difference? In the first exchange, the teacher is just venting. They are simply complaining in a way that does little but generate negative energy. The second teacher is confronted with the exact same challenge, but they deal with it constructively. They identify a problem, but do not dwell on it; they are trying to offer a positive path forward. The first teacher might be in a bad mood for the rest of the day. The second teacher isn't giving it another thought. The way that teachers deal with adversity throughout the day really does matter. I was attending a conference in Chicago in 2007 and heard Pedro Noguera proclaim, "If you believe the solution lies elsewhere, you render yourself irrelevant to the solution." When teachers are able to embrace their own potential to solve problems, when they are able to keep those problems in perspective, when they are able to maintain a positive attitude during the work day—in spite of the adversity—it can go a long way toward helping other teachers in the school to do the same.

Use Public Spaces Wisely

Every teacher has experienced it: listening to teachers gossip in the faculty lounge, complain at the lunch table, or even vent in the main office. And we certainly have all been guilty of this at various times in our career. We should resolve to quit. The energy that teachers bring into the school is palpable. The vibes that we all give off have an unmistakable impact. When we are negative, those around us are much more likely to become negative. But, by the same token, when we remain upbeat and commit to staying positive around our colleagues, we are contributing to the collective emotional well-being of the entire staff. We all have bad days, and we all need to vent from time to time, but remember that the culture in the building will be stronger when you make a point to vent privately to a single colleague. When you are with a group, it is the perfect time to get to know one another, learn from one another, and inspire one another. Use the public spaces in your school for collaborating, not for complaining.

Observe Other Teachers

In Chapter 4, we talked about the professional benefit derived from teachers observing their peers. The value of this experience extends beyond what you might learn, however. It can validate the teacher you are observing. It increases the level of respect between you and your colleague. It builds camaraderie. And it can strengthen your own confidence in the classroom. These are all benefits that have a positive impact on your own attitude at work.

Have Fun at Work

Teaching is your job; it is definitely work. Even when you are passionate, teaching can be a grind. But that does not mean you can't have fun while you're in the school building. In Chapter 2, we talked about how a teacher who is willing to let their guard down with students can have a positive impact in the classroom. The same is true for the way teachers can make a difference in the climate of the school. So, play practical jokes. Engage in shenanigans. Don't be afraid to be silly with your colleagues. Laughter does not just make you happy; it makes those around you happy.

If you're a teacher, it's in your DNA to make a difference! You are hardwired for significance. You are usually aware of the difference you make with kids, but never forget the difference you make with adults. You say and do things on a daily basis that transcend your classroom and, indeed, shape the culture of your school. The values, attitudes, and behaviors that you bring to work can inspire your colleagues, they can reinforce the core values of the school, and they can enhance the collective efforts of all those in the building who are working to make the school's vision a reality. Teachers do not just make a difference in their classroom; they make a difference in the culture of the entire school.

In the course of my career, I've had the privilege of working with various colleagues who truly loved their job. They engaged with students and truly cared about our school and everyone in it. When you have colleagues like this, it can be such a breath of fresh air. Having colleagues like this made me feel "on fire" and it made me want to become the best version of my "teacher" self, for my administrator but more importantly for my students. Being around someone who is always fueling the positivity vibes in the school makes for an amazing school culture. Choose to surround yourself with colleagues who can always find the silver lining; it will make you a happier person. **Positivity is contagious!**

When other teachers see you connect with the students and have fun at work, it makes for a happy environment for everyone. When students know their teacher truly cares about them and rocks the positive vibes, it rubs off! Be happy, be energetic, connect with your students, compliment their outfit, go to that football game to see them play, learn their silly TikTok dance. Don't hesitate to say I'm sorry when you are wrong. Those little things make a huge difference. Be that teacher who your colleagues and students enjoy being around!

Elise Skellie, Teacher

As I began the first day of my teaching career, my new "teacher wife" shared this phrase with me: "**Positivity is the key to success.**" I smiled, but did not truly understand that phrase until I was handed new curriculum guides, a large class size, a lunch wave that began at 10:15, the dreaded duty and committee schedule, and a stack of portfolios to peruse before those sweet second grade faces became mine in just a few short days. Then it hit me… That one simple phrase spoke volumes! You see, you cannot always change your circumstances, but you can always change how you react to them.

As I went through the years in three wonderful systems, I came to realize that I had the ability not only to change my outlook on things, but I could be a cheerleader for others. I knew that if I wanted to see a positive school culture, I had to be a team player and help cultivate that positivity with teachers and students. I used this positive outlook to help guide students to achieve their goals and my co-teachers to achieve theirs through PLCs, data, and collaboration meetings. All it took was an ear for listening, a hand for a high-five, a breakout cheer, or just a simple smile. These small gestures produced the positive energy needed to foster a strong school culture. Soon after, Positive Polly became my new name. Even now, as a K-12 instructional coach, the game is still the same, but the players are different. I am still Positive Polly as I continue to support teachers in reaching their goals. Is it easy? NO! Is it worth every strategic thought before I enter a classroom? YES! Anyone can be that positive energy of his or her school. If success is what you are looking for, shift your mindset.

Michele L. Bargman, Teacher

About 12 years into my teaching career, a colleague and I began discussing the need to see other teachers in their classrooms. After much discussion, we were determined to establish a system of teacher-led instructional rounds at our school, even if we were the only two participants. After an overwhelming response from our faculty, we implemented Leading by Learning teacher-led instructional rounds so that our teachers could learn and grow together. Small groups of teachers observed other teachers' lessons, and upon leaving the room, the groups reflected on the lessons and discussed methods of implementation for their own classrooms.

I was hooked after my first-ever observation. As my group of three stepped into Mrs. Dalton's tenth-grade English class, I was mesmerized by the large group discussion known as a "fishbowl" taking place in room H-256. Her desks were arranged with two concentric circles, and the students, not the teacher, were leading the discussion about a book called *The Turn of the Screw*. From the outside ring of desks, a student asked, "If the ghosts were real, why did the governess assume they had evil intent?" The students in the inner ring immediately began to hash out the governess's reasons. I was fascinated as we listened to tenth-graders passionately debating events from the book. As we walked toward our next observation, we discussed how to incorporate the fishbowl discussion into our science, math, and history classrooms. With every observation and reflection, my pedagogy strengthened as I filled my instructional toolbox with new approaches, techniques, and strategies.

Teachers are charged with the responsibility of inspiring, empowering, and growing students. We must also foster the growth of others in the profession. The numerous demands placed on teachers leave little time or incentive to learn from others; consequently, we risk stagnation in a profession vitally dependent upon creativity and innovation. Programs that cultivate collaboration can strengthen the profession and help nurture a community of life-long learners striving for excellence right alongside the students. And as teachers, we don't have to wait for the administration to set up collaborative opportunities for us. We can build a collaborative culture by simply taking steps to connect with teachers in our buildings.

Jennifer Brown, Educator

Conclusion

Recall our analogy to the medical profession. When we go to the doctor, we hope they know what they are talking about. We hope they diagnose us properly and prescribe the correct treatment. But this typically isn't accomplished if they do not take the time to listen to us, to truly understand what we are experiencing. And, if we are actually in the hospital, we hope the staff that attend to us enjoys their work, and that they show us genuine care.

Likewise, students deserve competent teachers. But "competent" is actually a low bar. I believe students deserve the "passionately committed" teachers described by Zehm and Kotler (1993): "Passionately committed teachers are those who absolutely love what they do. They are constantly searching for more effective ways to reach their children, to master the content and methods of their craft." (118) Students deserve to be in classrooms with teachers whose professional commitment compels them to plan, organize, and deliver lessons that will prepare them to be successful. But they also want teachers who will engage with them and care about them on a personal level. They want teachers who enjoy their job and make being in their classroom an enjoyable experience. Students want the type of passionate teacher described by Christopher Day (2004): "All effective teachers have a passion for their subject, a passion for their pupils and a passionate belief that who they are and how they teach can make a difference in their pupils' lives." (12)

If you have taught for a while, you have undoubtedly seen various courses of study come and go. You have seen academic standards change, and then change again. You have experienced the evolution of pedagogy with trends that include cooperative learning, differentiated instruction, and problem-based learning. Technological innovations have included everything from mechanical pencils, to film strip projectors, to interactive "smart" boards. Clearly, there is much that changes in education. But there is one thing that never changes: the practices of great teachers: they manage their room; they cultivate a healthy climate in that room; they are thoughtful with the instructional process; they are relentless about their own professional growth; they stay grounded in their core purpose; they take time to understand and know their students; they build relationships with those students; and they embrace their ability to foster a strong culture within the school building.

My two sons had the same favorite teacher in high school. (It also happened to be the hardest class they ever took!) She was their AP Chemistry teacher and they talked about her all the time. Finally, I asked my younger son what made her such a good teacher. I expected a response something like this: "Dad, do you know how smart she is? She has a Ph.D.!", or "She's really good at explaining things," or "She has great relationships with her students." But that is not what I got. His response caught me off guard when he said, "Dad, she cares so much about her job." But it was obvious to my sons that it was so much more to her than just a "job;" it was her passion.

So teachers, thank you for caring about your job. And thank you for making it your passion. Your students notice; your colleagues notice, and, quite often, the parents do as well. It is your passion for being an effective teacher that allows you to make the difference you do. Teaching is a wonderful career; thank you for making it yours.

Epilogue

The Fourth Dimension: Teacher Self-Care

I already know what a child needs. I know it by heart. He needs to be accepted, respected, liked, and trusted; encouraged, supported, activated and amused; able to explore, experiment and achieve. Damn it! He needs too much. All I lack is Solomon's wisdom, Freud's insight, Einstein's knowledge, and Florence Nightingale's dedication.

(33–34)

Haim Ginott quotes this teacher in his best seller, *Teacher and Child*, published in 1972. I am sure this frustration—this emotional burden—still resonates with many teachers as I write these words almost 50 years later. In recent years, various books and articles have been written to address the need for teacher self-care. Jenny Grant Rankin, for example, offers sobering statistics about the stressful realities of teachers in her book *First Aid for Teacher Burnout* (2017). Cabeen, Johnson, and Johnson (2018) write, "With the heavy burden in the workplace, educators often arrive home, emotionally and physically exhausted, and then feel guilty for never having enough or being enough to fully engage at home. (xv) And as Day (2004) noted, "almost all teachers will face a time when the well of passion runs dry." (159) Most of us have heard stories about teachers who leave the profession after only a few years, or we have heard about the numbers of teachers who report high levels of job-related stress. There is no way of getting around it—teaching is stressful. It is not a job for the faint of heart. Educators frequently talk about the pervasive mental health concerns with our students; but we also need to be mindful of the mental health of our teachers.

In *Hacking Teacher Burnout*, Amber Harper discusses eight strategies for teachers to retain professional fulfillment while navigating the stresses of being a teacher. Cabeen et al. (2018) also provide strategies for maintaining a healthy work–home balance while still retaining one's passion. Springer, Alexander, and Persiani (2012) put it simply in *The Organized Teacher*: "Always monitor yourself and do not overextend your energies. Get lots of rest and leave as much work at work as you can." (x) It is imperative that teachers learn to take care of themselves. They need to make their own mental health a priority. Spend time with family and friends; cultivate a professional learning network through social media—not just for the professional learning, but for the support and camaraderie. In the final analysis, I think one of the most important strategies is embodied in Chapter 5 of this book. As Day (2004) put it, teachers need to "revisit core values and beliefs regularly." (177) In my experience, this is the best way to remain inspired: remain mindful of what led you into this profession; ultimately, it will be what sustains you in this profession.

References

Anderson, L.W. & Krathwohl, D.R. (2001) A Taxonomy for Learning, Teaching, and Assessing: A Revision of Bloom's Taxonomy of Educational Objectives. Longman.

Beck, A.E. (1994). On universities: J. Tuzo Wilson Medal acceptance speech. Elements: Newsletter of the Canadian Geophysical Union, 12, 7–9.

Bloom, B.S. (1956). Taxonomy of Educational Objectives, Handbook 1: Cognitive Domain. Longman.

Burgess, D. (2012). Teach Like a Pirate: Increase Student Engagement, Boost Your Creativity, and Transform Your Life as an Educator. Dave Burgess Consulting, Inc.

Cabeen, J., Johnson, J., & Johnson, S. (2018). Balance Like a Pirate: Going Beyond Work-Life Balance to Ignite Passion and Thrive as an Educator. Dave Burgess Publishing.

"Culturally Responsive Teaching: A Reflection Guide." (2020 September, 23). New America. www.newamerica.org/education-policy/policy-papers/culturally-responsive-teaching-competencies/.

Day, C. (2004) A Passion for Teaching. RoutledgeFalmer.

Dufour, R. (2004, May). What is a professional learning community? Educational Leadership, 61(8), 6–11. Retrieved from http://www.ascd.org/publications/educational-leadership/may04/vol61/num08/What-Is-a-Professional-Learning-Community%C2%A2.aspx

Dufour, R., Dufour, R., Eaker, R., & Many, T. (2010). Learning by Doing: A Handbook for Professional Learning Communities at Work. Solution Tree Press.

Eisely, L.C. (1978). Retrieved from http://www.starfishlearning.com/cms2/the-starfish-story/

Gay, G. (2000). Culturally Responsive Teaching: Theory, Research, and Practice. Teachers College Press.

Ginott, H. (1972). Teacher and Child: A Book for Parents and Teachers. Macmillan.

Gorski, P. (2018). Reaching and Teaching Students in Poverty: Strategies for Erasing the Opportunity Gap. 2nd ed. Teacher's College Press.

Hattie, J.A.C. (2009). Visible Learning: A Synthesis of 800+ Meta-Analyses on Achievement. Routledge.

Hattie, J.A.C. (2012). Visible Learning for Teachers: Maximizing Impact on Learning. Routledge.

Knight, J. (2011). Unmistakable Impact: A Partnership Approach for Dramatically Improving Instruction. Corwin.

Ladson-Billings, G. (1994). The Dreamkeepers: Successful Teachers of African-American Children. Jossey-Bass.

Marzano, R. (2003). What Works in Schools: Translating Research into Action. ASCD.

Maslow, A.H. (1943). A theory of human motivation. Psychological Review, 50(4), 370–396.

Mooney, T. (2018). Why We Say "Opportunity Gap" instead of "Achievement Gap". Retrieved from https://www.teach-foramerica.org/stories/why-we-say-opportunity-gap-instead-of-achievement-gap

Muñiz, J. (2020a). Culturally Responsive Teaching: A Reflection Guide. New America.

Muñiz, J. (2020b). Culturally Responsive Teaching: A Reflection Guide. New America.

Nesloney, T. & Welcome, A. (2016). Kids Deserve It!: Pushing Boundaries and Challenging Conventional Thinking. Dave Burgess Publishing

Pink, D.H. (2009). Drive: The Surprising Truth about What Motivates Us. Riverhead Books.

Prenski, M. (2001, October). Digital Natives. Digital Immigrants: A New Way to Look at Ourselves and Our Kids. On the Horizon (pp. 1–6). Vol. 9, No. 5. NCB University Press.

Rankin, J.G. (2017). First Aid for Teacher Burnout. Routledge.

Rebora, A. (2008, September 10). Making a Difference. Education Week Teacher PD Sourcebook.

Robert, M. (2003) What Works in Schools: Translating Research into Action. ASCD.

Schlechty, P. (2002) Working on the Work: An Action Plan for Teachers, Principals, and Superintendents. Jossey-Bass.

Schlechty, P. (2011). Engaging Students: The Next Level of Working on the Work. Jossey-Bass.

Schweig, J., Hamilton, L.S., & Baker, G. (2019). School and Classroom Climate Measures: Considerations for Use by State and Local Education Leaders. Research report by Rand Corporation.

Sheehy, R. (2018) Be the One for Kids. Dave Burgess Publishing.

Sinek, S. (2011). Start with Why: How Great Leaders Inspire Everyone to Take Action. Penguin Books.

Springer, S., Alexander, B., & Persiani, K. (2012). The Organized Teacher: A Hands on Guide to Setting Up and Running a Terrific Classroom. McGraw Hill.

Steele, D. Steele Thoughts: The Reflection of an Educator. Retrieved from http://www.steelethoughts.com.

Steele, D. (2019). The Challenge: Maintaining Staff Morale. In Zoul, J. & Bell, S. (Eds.), Education Write Now, Volume III: Solutions to Common Challenges in Your School or Classroom (pp. 155–168). Routledge.

Steele, D. & Whitaker, T. (2019). Essential Truths for Teachers. Routledge.

Stronge, James H. & Xu, Xianxuan (2016) Instructional Planning for Effective Teaching. Solution Tree Press.

Tomlinson, C. (2017) How to Differentiate Instruction in Academically Diverse Classrooms. 3rd ed. ASCD.

Tomlinson, C. & McTighe, J. (2006). Integrating Differentiated Instruction + Understanding by Design. ASCD.

Wang, M., Haertel, G, & Walberg, H. (December 1993/January 1994). Synthesis of Research: What Helps Students Learn. Educational Leadership, 51(4), 74–79.

Webb, N. (1997) Research Monograph no. 6. A Criteria for Alignment of Expectations and Assessments in Mathematics and Science Education. National Institute for Science Education: University of Wisconsin-Madison.

Whitaker, T. (2020a) What Great Principals Do Differently: Twenty Things That Matter Most. Routledge.

Whitaker, T. (2020b). What Great Teachers Do Differently, 3rd Edition: Nineteen Things That Matter Most. Routledge.

Whitaker, T., Zoul, J., & Casas, J. (2015). What Connected Educators Do Differently. Routledge.

Wong, H.K. & Wong, R.T. (2005). First Days of School: How to be an Effective Teacher. Harry K. Wong Publications, Inc.

Wormeli, R. (2006, Summer). Accountability: Teaching Through Assessment and Feedback, Not Grading. American Secondary Education 34(3). 14–27.

Wormeli, R. (2015, October) The Seven Habits of Highly Affective Educators. Vol. 73, No. 2, (10–15). Educational Leadership.

Zehm, S.J. & Kotler, J.A. (1993). On Being a Teacher: The Human Dimension. Corwin Press, Inc.